MEN ARE USELESS

A slightly embellished account of

women's relationships with men

ELLIE RUSSO

AUTHOR'S NOTES

Some useless men's names have been changed to protect the women in their lives from certain lawsuits. Others are real because – what the hell, why not?

Content Warning:

This book contains explicit content and sensitive themes, including scenes of sexual activity, consumption of alcohol and drugs, use of inappropriate language, and instances of violence. Reader discretion is advised.

Get In Touch:

ellierussomen@gmail.com

To all the women who love the useless men,

I've loved before.

CONTENTS

INTRODUCTION 1

1 DEAR OLD DAD 4

Daddy's Girl No More

Natasha's Father

Ava's Dad

Jackie's Dads

Deadbeat Duds

2 SOMETIMES YOU'VE GOT TO KISS A FEW FROGS 30

Boys in Men's Clothing

Heeeeere's Johnny

3 HUSBAND NUMBER ONE – FATHER OF MY FIRST TWO 41

Hooray – It's Wine Release Saturday!

4 HUSBAND NUMBER TWO – THE MISTAKE ON THE TAKE 47

5 OTHER WOMEN'S HUSBANDS 53

Liz's Procrastinator

Lory's Two-Timing Timmy

Bob 'The Knob'

6 SEPARATION – LET THE (HEAD) GAMES BEGIN 65

Emily's Story (in her own words)

Single Dads vs. Single Moms

Jan's Man

Out Of The Marriage, But Not Out Of The House

Lyla's Losers

And Then There's Todd

7 SAD SACKS 76

I Can't Get No...

He's All That...

Cecilia's Sex Education

The 6 Million Dollar, 2 Second Man

8 THE SONS OF US BITCHES! 81

Wife, Mom – It's All the Same in Sickness!

Spoiled / Rotten

Mad Max

A Truly Bad Seed

9 BROTHERS NEED MANY MOTHERS 95

Dinner With Jay

"Baby" Brothers

Life Is Tougher "Up Here"

10 HORRIBLE BOSSES 101

The Bad, The Good, And the F'ugly

doG, ssoB - It's All The Same In A Dyslexic And Dysfunctional Workplace

My First But Not My Last

The Ageists

Bills to Pay, People to Sue

New Job, New Hope, New Set of Micromanaging Headaches

(Real) Letters to My Editors

Re: The Micromanager

Re: The Bully

To: The Narcissists

Maggie's Megalomaniac

Adriana's Notorious P.I.G.

11 THE TEENAGE DAUGHTER YEARS   125

Julia (Jules)

Ella ("Goo")

12 TWENTY- FIVE YEARS TO DEAD – THE ART OF LONG-LASTING MARRIAGE 135

The (Not So) Classic Hollywood Marriage

13 EVEN ON THE BIG SCREEN, MEN ARE USELESS   140

14 POST-DIVORCE DATING   143

Good Guys Want Tough Girls

Time To Moving On, Not In

15 YOUNG LOVES   152

My "Beau"

Alex

Serra's Married Young Man

16 MAMA'S BOYS – FACE IT, WE WILL NEVER MEASURE UP!   161

Bella's Bambino

Babcia's Boy

Finally, Tara's Time

17 ONLINE DATING – IT JUST "LOL's" ME OUT!   169

"LOL"

The "Good Guy" Profile

Meet You At The Bar

The "Rules" of Online Dating

Alma's 50 Shades of Fuckin' Eh!

When Fishing Season Was Officially Over

18 POSERS, BREADCRUMBERS, AND CATFISH – OH MY!   186

POSERS

The Fat Bank Account Trick

BREADCRUMBERS
   Poetic Justice
   When in Rome

CATFISH
   Just Do It!
   The Happy Ending
   Double Duped

19 GIRLS JUST WANNA HAVE FUN   **202**

Pat's Penance

Joyce's Jolly Jerk

20 USELESS MEN IN POLITICS   **208**

Only In America

Canadians Aren't Much Better, Eh?

21 BAD INFLUENCES   **214**

Andrew Tate

FreshandFit

22 EQUALITY AND THE USELESS MAN   **220**

Misogyny Hates Company

Sherry's Chivalrous-less Chumps
   Mr. Cheap And Charmless
   Mr. Chivalry For A Select Few

23 EMBARRASSMENT IS WORSE THAN USELESSNESS   **228**

Jarrod's Holiday "Uniform"

Another Jarrod Classic

24 GREAT UNCLES   **233**

Uncle Terry:

Uncle Hal:

Adventures With Uncle Jay
   Send In The Clowns
   KFC Anyone?
   Never Gonna Give, Never Gonna Give ...

25 THE BOYS IN MY HOOD (AKA "PETER PANDAS")   240

26 PICKING MY BATTLES   243

Side-Walking - The Social Experiment

Karen and Her Husband

27 FRIENDS' IN "HIGH" PLACES   250

Sid n' Nancy

Kurt and Courtney

Bonnie and Clyde

28 MEN WHO ARE "JUST FRIENDS"   257

29 THE PERFECT MAN...   259

30 WOMEN ARE FAR FROM USELESS   261

INTRODUCTION

Men are useless. It's harsh perhaps, but true. This declaration does not come from some irreparably scorned woman, or crazy cat lady who has no use for our less fair gender. It comes from experience - too much in fact, with those whose contributions to my life and the lives of countless other women, have been little more than occupying space on the couch, at our dinner tables, and most often, in our bleeding hearts. Don't get me wrong, I'm not a member of the *"Man Haters Unite"* club. It's quite the contrary. I love men. I love the way they walk, their manly-man ruggedness, their self-confidence, their filthy senses of humour, and especially the way they smell. And, if a man happens to have some good facial hair and a great sense of style, I'm toast.

It's just that... some guys are lazy, while others are self-absorbed. Some guys play childish mind games, and some are cheaters or they're cheap (or both). Many men have no clue or desire to learn how to please a woman in or out of bed, and surprisingly, some have absolutely zero competence when it comes to looking after their own kids. And other men, for a myriad of reasons that I will share with you in the coming pages, are just plain useless!

In a girl's time on this earth, we go through many phases and rites of passage. We enter puberty and get our periods, we meet and get crushes on boys (or girls), and we go on countless bad dates. Sometimes we get married. And sometimes, we get divorced. 100% of the time, we're the only ones who give birth, and sadly as we age, and head towards our "golden years," we're rewarded with the extreme discomfort and dullness of menopause. These life stages are tests and testaments to our unwavering drive to survive. But they also offer life lessons that help us to thrive in a big bad man's world.

Now that I am older, and much wiser, having breezed through these unforgettable phases (some more than once), I prefer to think of these experiences as a woman's movement toward "the light." As we earn our scars and gripes, we take one step closer to enlightenment. Remember the scene in the old scary movie *Poltergeist*, when the little ghost-wrangler woman says, *"Go into the light. There is peace and serenity in the light"*? I think she was trying to give us girls a warning . . . to wake up and smell the survival coffee (or vino, when the coffee's not cutting it anymore), and realize that men will never change. They will always be from Mars, bars, or man caves, and as such, they are very, very different from us. While it's true that men are useless, we still need them, and only by discovering and embracing our men versus women realities, will we ever truly be free.

A while back, I visited my brother Ryan (Ry) and his ex-wife, Jenn. Yes, you read that correctly - the "exes" together. Remarkably, they have remained great friends and until recently, they spent far too much time together - at her place, of course. Upon entry, I saw my brother, lying on her sofa, in Jenn's pink fluffy bathrobe, watching her Netflix, chowing down on food from her well-stocked fridge, and of course, ignoring their two extremely energetic young boys. At that moment, I saw my baby brother in a brand-new light. And man, was it dim! He was no longer just my funny, handsome, oh-so-charming, and fun brother. Rather, he was a useless, lazy, self-important jerk.

Upon sharing my thoughts with his very tolerant and almost doting "ex," she started to spill her guts. For the first time, it's as though she had been given validation of her feelings, and a real opportunity to vent. It was okay for her to acknowledge that he was useless, and undeserving of one more minute of the free ride he'd long enjoyed, at her expense. At that moment, I was determined to see to it that my brother's lady-bathrobe-wearing, Netflix & food-binging, and kid-ignoring ways, were about to end – whether he liked it or not.

As the night progressed, Jenn and I sufficiently ignored my brother, while he ignored us and his children. It was a great, productive night. We had a long and heartfelt chat about all the men in (and out of) our lives, and together, we discovered that each man, in his own way, has had a profound impact on us. Over a good bottle of Californian cabernet sauvignon, we formulated an outline for this book, ensuring to "honour" all those who have graced us with their uselessness.

That night was a while ago, and this book has been a long time in the making. I knew that I needed to do the title justice, so I took my sweet time (years in fact), and I interviewed lots (and lots) of women. Whether in person or online, I've held hundreds of fascinating conversations with female friends, friends of friends, close and distant relatives, co-workers, and even a city bus driver. In this journey, I've gathered some hilarious and disturbing stories and a lifetime of gloriously dirty details.

Some anecdotes are old now, some are new, and some are slightly exaggerated - but all are based on real women's very real experiences with men. Over the years, in my quest to find the ultimate *Men Are Useless* story, I discovered a universal truth: Every woman has one. Here are some of my old and new favourites.

1

DEAR OLD DAD

*"I cannot think of any need in childhood as strong
as the need for a father's protection." - Sigmund Freud*

When I remember my upbringing, it's no small wonder why I've been drawn to useless men. I think most women are conditioned towards this path from early childhood. Think about it - after enduring many long months and torturous hours of labour, just to bring us into this world, our moms are expected to snap right back into a machine-like mode, like Arnold's *Terminator,* and take on the endless and exhausting job of feeding us, burping us, clothing us, bathing us, changing our poopy diapers, and waking up to our loud cries, countless times in the night - only to begin the exhausting routine all over again, the next sleepless day.

But where are the dads in all this infant-rearing non-bliss? My own father was far too busy and important to be involved in anything so trivial as caring for his infant children. His major contribution to the household was to take out the trash once a week and shovel the snow in the winter. That was it. That is, until I got old enough to do it for him. Seriously!

My dad's main job at home was to fuel up on all the wholesome and homemade hot meals that my working mom could serve him, and be sure to get plenty of uninterrupted sleep, in anticipation of the 'exhausting' workday ahead at his big corner office, executive job, located just 10 short minutes from our house. During the warmer months (April to early November to be exact), a twice-weekly trip to the golf club was also mandatory to help keep his daily stress at bay.

When it came to our comfortable home life, I couldn't give my mom all the credit, though. Having grown up as a child of privilege with hired help to cook, clean, and assist her with her "chores," my mother was more comfortable giving direction, than playing the martyr. For this reason, she was only too pleased to pass on her limited domestic abilities to my sister and me, in the hope that we'd embrace and improve upon the tradition of serving the men in our lives. By passing this torch, my mom was effectively pigeonholing us into domestic engineering misery so that we, in turn, could ignite a fire under the next female generation, to carry on the tradition of devoting themselves to male servitude.

I am the second born of four kids, and technically a middle child. I have an older sister and two younger brothers. Around the age of 10, I learned what it was to be "Daddy's best girl." Every weekday morning around 7 a.m., my dad would make the trip down the hallway to the bedroom I shared with my sister. He is half Italian and half Irish – and he explained that this is the reason he always yelled. This was my morning alarm; *"Girls, girls get up, and get your brothers ready for school. Make sure their hair is combed, they've had their breakfast, and their teeth are brushed before you walk them to school."*

It didn't stop there. I must have been pretty good at the caretaking thing, because by age 12, in addition to caring for the grooming needs of my grubby brothers, I was also making most of the family meals, taking out the trash, cleaning the house, and even cutting the grass - all while my pathetic little brothers sat on their skinny asses in front of the TV, with my useless dad. Somehow, my clearly smarter, older sister, Anne, managed to come up with pseudo-ailments like severe allergies and chronic colds, to keep the chores off her plate, and piling up on mine.

When questioned by a neighbour one hot summer day, as to why his daughter was the one always cutting the grass when he had two healthy boys at home, my father laughingly replied, *"Oh, haven't you met Ellie? She's the son I never had."* The two men shared a knowing, demeaning chuckle, and I got back to the weed whacker. While the neighbour's observation should have made me furious, in some twisted way, it made me feel proud. I had worked so hard, and for so long, and now I was good enough to be called "son."

So, if cooking, cleaning, cutting grass, and looking after my brothers weren't enough to make the neighbours want to sick Children's Protective Services on my parents, then the experience that my family still laughingly refers to as, "*A penny a bucket*," certainly is.

Me, my siblings, and my mom, spent every full summer at our family cottage - a cute little gray bungalow on the tip of a tiny eight-cottage island in Muskoka, Ontario. My mom was an interior design teacher at the local community college, so she was "as free as a bird" for the two-plus summer months that she effectively held my siblings and I hostage, on our little Island. My dad stayed at home during the week, as he had to work. However, he would make the one-and-a-half-hour drive north each weekend and spend his entire "visit" yelling at us for not doing more around the cottage.

Every year, about two weeks into our rather sheltered summer holiday, my brothers and I devolved into wild animals - just like Mowgli from The Jungle Book. We were happiest running around like savages in our perpetually shoeless, unkempt, and dirty state. My sister was somehow afforded the luxury of sleeping in until 3 p.m. daily. More days than not, she would awake complaining about all the noise we were making. She was not at all a bullfrog-catching explorer like the rest of us, so we just ignored her and carried on with our daily jungle routine.

The summer I turned 13 was particularly memorable for me - not because I was heading into the glory of young womanhood, or because I'd even had my first kiss with Tommy Dawson, the son of one of my mom's visiting friends. No, this was the summer that I helped my dad build a giant break wall around the front of our lakefront property. Its purpose was to prevent the weakened ground from eroding and to help keep our much-loved little cottage from sinking into the lake. I always worked very hard for my dad because I'd have done anything to get him to appreciate me and give me a little pat on the back.

That summer, my father enlisted me to help him – well by him, I mean a young man he hired to do my dad's heavy lifting - with the break wall. My job was to drag a large, square metal bucket through the lake to the most shallow and sandy part. Then, using a shovel, I would fill the bucket as high as I could with sand. I would then drag the sand-filled bucket back to the meshed support structure, and pour the sand in. Each bucketful must have weighed about 40 pounds – a little less than half of what I weighed at the time. The young man that my dad hired to help with the monstrous project, was available only on Saturdays and Sundays, and his job was to secure the mesh around the break wall, and pile rocks on top of my watery sand deposits.

Day upon gruelling day, I worked at the break wall, while my brothers caught frogs in the swamp, my mom painted watercolour landscapes on the front deck of the cottage, and my sister tanned herself on the dock all day, like an iguana. Even when my dad went home for the week, I kept up the pace, hoping to surprise him with my progress, when he'd return the following weekend.

When he came back to the island each Friday evening, he was indeed impressed with the evidence of my hard work. A cottaging neighbour popped by to tell my dad that he should be extremely proud of me as he'd watched me daily with amazement from his own dock, drag bucket after bucket of water-soaked sand to the edge of the property – lift, pour and repeat, with all my wiry might.

As I kept on working, pretending not to hear what the men were saying about my excellent work ethic, I heard the neighbour, Mr. Russell, ask my dad how much he was paying me for this huge job that was clearly intended for a big, strong man, and not some young skinny teenage girl. To this, my dad sheepishly replied, *"Ya' know, we haven't worked it out yet, but she's doing a great job, and I'm sure she'll have a nice little savings by the end of the summer."*

Standing knee-deep in cloudy lake water, I turned to the two men who were about ten feet away. I was anxious to stick up for my dad because I felt that Mr. Russell (like everyone else who had witnessed my verging-on-child-abuse work schedule) was insinuating that my dad was taking advantage of me. I proudly announced, *"Mr. Russell, I'm getting paid a penny a bucket. I'm up to one dollar and seventy-eight cents now."* With that, Mr. Russell turned on his heels, and quickly walked back to his cottage, without saying another word to any of us for the rest of the summer.

In looking back on that experience, it's now clear that my dad was not only useless, but he was also not child abuse-less either. Please don't feel sorry for me, though, as I managed to achieve retribution for my dad's treatment of me as a kid. For many years into my adulthood when my father had become a big deal in the Canadian college system, and later within the legal world, I would take great pride in retelling this story every time I was in his mixed company of friends and colleagues, just for the cruel delight of seeing the shocked look on their faces, and the shame in his eyes.

Daddy's Girl No More

Upon completing my first, very rough draft of *Men Are Useless*, I asked an acquaintance, and now dear friend, to review my writing and tell me what he honestly thought of the book. Being a talented author, and accomplished film director, with a wicked sense of humour, I knew that Pete would give it to me straight. He told me that although he knew for a fact that I adore men and that I meant for this book to be mostly tongue-in-cheek, the tone was coming across as more than a tad bit bitter. He believed that my only honest bit of self-reflective writing was when I spoke about my relationship with my dad as a young kid. The rest was just funny, man-bashing satire.

After his critique, I decided to revisit my stories and make them as real and self-reflective as I possibly could, so as not to cheat the reader or my real self. With a deep breath, I am sharing the rest of my story as it pertains to my dad, so that you may come to understand how I got myself involved with an ensuing slew of useless men.

About twenty-five years ago, my dad had an affair. The "other woman" was a doting divorcee who worked at arm's-length with my father in an executive role, at a community college. At the time, my dad was well into several decades of marriage to my mom, but quite obviously, he was long out of marital bliss. He had just accepted a job in Toronto, which meant that he'd be spending his weekdays in the big city, while his not-so-little family remained living an hour north, in our hometown. As for his doting divorcee, she poured the charm on thick, and he loved the attention. It was about that time that he began dreading his weekend trips "home" to his demanding and tired wife, and the dad duties he felt forced to assume, for his four demanding (and sometimes downright unlawful) teenage kids.

Having recently sold our Muskoka cottage - you know, the one we adored so much – to be able to afford the purchase of a luxury penthouse condo on the Toronto Harbourfront, we were all more than a little resentful that he'd traded in our summer slice of family togetherness, for his own, personal big-city haven. Accepting that our summers would no longer involve cottage life, we embraced the idea of summer weekends at the four-bedroom glass palace in the Toronto skyline, close to cool concert venues, great restaurants, and amazing attractions.

My dad, unfortunately, had other ideas. He was determined to keep the pristine place that my interior designer mother had tastefully but sparsely decorated, all to himself. He did everything in his power to keep us all away, including funding (and signing a 3-year lease for) a retail interior design showroom for my mom in our hometown. This would ensure that my mom's hands and roots were tied to a business and life, a hundred miles away from him. He also made his teenage kids get summer jobs, close to home. It was settled – my father would be the only Torontonian in the family, and he even instructed the concierge of "our" luxury condo, not to let us in, unless he was there.

So much for reaping the rewards of his accomplished career, and the outlandish profit he made from the sale of our beloved family cottage. We were now cottage-less and left to, no, I mean guilted into, looking after our mother, who could clearly sense the distance (both emotionally and physically) between her and my dad.

When I discovered the affair - and I do mean "I," that was the beginning of the end for me, and the relationship with the man whose approval once meant my world. I remember the discovery very clearly. It was the summer after my first year of university. I had just turned 20 and was thrilled to have a few months off to connect with my old friends, none of whom attended the same post-secondary school that I did.

One Sunday night, I drove with my friends, one hour down Highway 400 to Toronto, to attend "Psychedelic Sundays" at RPM, a popular alternative nightclub at the time. On route to the club, which was located a mere two kilometres from my dad's place - ahem, I mean, my family's condo on the Toronto Harbourfront, we were stopped at a traffic light. From the passenger's seat, my friend Pam animatedly pointed towards a restaurant patio, beside us and said, *"Hey isn't that your dad, making out with some bleached blond?"*

The couple couldn't have been more than ten feet away from the car, and my mind was a million miles from Earth. It was confirmed. My dad, who shamelessly used to grope my mom's ass in public, was now cheating on the love of his life, with a much younger, chick named "Katie." He was deceiving his wife and kids, and he had just devastated me - the one who was so devoted and starved for his affection and approval. At the time, it felt almost too much to bear, as I knew that it was just a matter of time before my parents would separate.

After the shocking discovery, and in a complete fog, I somehow managed to keep driving, drop my friends at the nightclub, and head back up the highway, home to share the disturbing details of what I had discovered, with my mom. This decision was not easy, but it was the right thing to do, and thanks to my dad, I was feeling increasingly responsible for my mother's emotional health.

As I entered the house, my mom was "assuming her position," perched at her drafting table in one windowed corner of the family room, working on one of her many elaborate interior design sketches. When she saw the look on my face, she knew that something was up, and all was not right. I was far from my chipper self. I was home about five hours earlier than expected, and I could barely look her in the eyes.

The moment was almost surreal. Even before I spoke, she knew what I was about to tell her, and somehow, I knew that she would reject the truth. In an instant, I went from losing my useless father, to losing all respect for my loving, strong, and achingly honest mom. When I told her what I had seen, she told me that I must be mistaken, as she had spoken to my dad just minutes earlier, and he was attending a conference all weekend. I was also told that I should stop stirring up sh*t, just for attention. At that moment, I was kind of done with my mother too.

Until very recently, I had little, to no relationship with my father. It was always more "off" than "on," and we spoke awkwardly at rare all-inclusive family occasions. As I'd predicted so many years earlier, my father left my sad and devoted mother, and he married Katie. On the bright side, the couple seems happy together in their quiet twosome world of expensive homes and exclusive golf clubs - a six-bedroom main home on the water in a prestigious Toronto suburb, a five-bedroom summer home in my once-beloved cottage country, Muskoka, and a winter home I've never seen, nor have I been invited to, in Scottsdale, Arizona. They have memberships to golf clubs near each of these places, and their (6 combined) adult children, and piles of grandchildren, rarely visit. None of us are genuinely welcome in their tiny world – and some (ahem), are less so than others.

The possibility of igniting a real father-daughter relationship was all but extinguished for the final time when, several years back, I suffered a slight mental and emotional breakdown over my eldest daughter's self-destructive behaviour. At the time, I really (really) needed some help from family. My mother was not an option, as her emotional health was irreparably weakened since the divorce, and it was still my job to cater to her happiness. So, I swallowed my pride and reached out to my dad for some fatherly advice and emotional support. Sadly, I found none. He didn't want to get involved. He felt that my *"matter was private,"* meaning that my hardships were not his problem, nor his burden to take on. Again, this was almost too much to bear – but you know how the old saying goes; *"What doesn't kill us, makes us stronger."* And stronger, I certainly became – alone!

The troubles I experienced with my eldest daughter, were a few years ago, and everything is fine now, in my own little family. For this reason, I have tried to bury the hatchet with my dad, as best I can, without having to engage in any sort of deep conversation about our "relationship." Strangely, we now (coincidentally) live just 4

13

doors apart, on the same street – my youngest daughter and I live in a cute little cottage-like rental, and he and his wife are still in their 6-bedroom home for two. My older (now adult) kids have left the nest, for university.

I see my dad and his wife about once a year, and it usually involves me inviting them for dinner, to secure a family connection, albeit an awkward one. My youngest girl doesn't have much of a relationship with her grandfather either. She looks just like me when I was her age (she's now 15), and I think she's a painful reminder to my father of his poor parental choices.

There is still a strain between us, but my mental health has mended because I've learned to establish boundaries and put myself first in that so-called relationship. At this point in my life, I choose to be happy and grounded, because I need to be the best possible parent I can, to ensure that my own children feel loved and supported, and don't become mentally and emotionally f*%#@ed up.

Natasha's Father

Natasha's parents are Polish immigrants to Canada. They moved to Toronto just before she was born. Natasha recalls that while growing up, silence was golden - unless of course, you were a man and particularly one who liked to share a few nightly shots of "wodka" with the other Polish men from the neighbourhood. This nightly ritual included Natasha's much-adored, older brother, Ralph (pronounced 'Ra-fow,' in Polish). His inclusion meant that he felt and acted superior to Natasha, and their mother, Iwona.

Before hearing Natasha's story, I thought that my own mother had been worked to the bone by her job, her husband, and her kids.

14

Wow – was I wrong. In Natasha's home, serving men was a full-time job, and for the ladies of the house, this felt like a prison sentence. Natasha's father ran the roost, so to speak. His word was the first word in the house (her brother's, was a close second), and the women literally had to serve the men and work their asses off, just to buy themselves a little free time, to practice some much-needed self-care. By free time, I'm talking about being "let out" of the house to attend school and go to work.

Before and after school and work, Natasha and her mom were responsible for the household's daily chores, including cleaning the house, making, and serving the meals (to the men first, of course), and then clearing and cleaning the dishes. Trips to buy groceries and other home supplies were counted as free time. The women were also told when it was okay to speak and when to "bądź cicho kobieto" or "quiet down, woman!" To act with any independence, without first clearing a decision with "zee man," as Natasha's mother called her dad behind his back, was a surefire way to end up "grounded."

Natasha, who is now an adult and living on her own, is deliberately taking a break from men for a while. Since leaving "zee men" of her upbringing, she's naturally gravitated to controlling types – and experienced a few disastrous relationships of her own, that is, until she got a solid therapist, and found a sense of self-worth.

When I asked Natasha what her parents' relationship is like these days, she smiled and said, "The old guy has finally chilled out. He's not the oppressive taskmaster that he used to be." Now, he even takes his wife out for a nice dinner occasionally. As for her thirty-something, still-living-at-home brother, Ralph – he's predictably, unhappily single.

Ava's Dad

Recently, my friend Ava was chatting with her older brother, Tom, and they were not-so-fondly recalling their childhood. In trying to tally the number of outings they had with their father in their formative years, they agreed on a whopping total of between 3 and 5. Among their limited "wild" adventures with their dear old dad, day trips to the library and local used bookstores topped the list. As a university law professor and later, a secondhand bookstore owner, Mr. Fischer's idea of a good time was digging into a dusty old paperback and forgetting reality for a few hours. That, of course, meant not paying any real attention to his children.

One day at the library of the university where her dad worked, 4-year-old Ava decided she'd had enough of being told *"shhh"* by just about everyone she bothered for some (any) attention, especially her dad. So, she did what any attention-starved preschooler would do - she pulled a fire alarm. As the high ceilings rang with eardrum-breaking alarm bells, Ava jumped up and down in delight as people scurried by her, and frantically towards the exit doors – no one noticing the blue ink on her tiny right hand. The ink was her badge of dishonour, for pulling the alarm.

When Mr. Fischer deciphered what Ava had done, he scolded her and later vowed to his over-worked, under-appreciated wife, that he would no longer be graciously taking the children with him on his outings. Sadly, Ava shared with me, that this was about the only promise her dad ever kept when it came to his neglected kids.

On a happier note, Ava's dad's behaviour wasn't nearly as disgraceful as her brother-in-law's. She recounted that Darren, her sister, Wendy's husband, who was a chronic gambler (he may still be, but he and Wendy are divorced now), often took his young daughter and son, unbeknown to his wife, to the racetrack with him on Saturday afternoons. His wife, Wendy thought she was being given a much-needed rest, when in fact, Darren was using the kids as a beard for his addiction to the ponies.

On those fateful Saturday afternoons, the children had to wait patiently in the car for 2 hours or more, parked at the far corner of the raceway parking lot. The reason for this was to ensure that no bystanders caught a glimpse of them and to prevent any possible stranger danger. Depending on the outcome of the races, Max and Maddie would either get a treat at Dairy Queen, or they'd have to continue sitting on a curb while their dad drowned his sorrows inside a nearby dive bar for the rest of the afternoon.

Ava's sister Wendy also recalled her childhood memories of their father. Like her sister Ava, on the rare occasion that she was invited to spend time with her father, it was usually in front of the TV, watching some lame sports game, although these moments were almost always marked by near silence. Occasionally, if his team was winning, Wendy would get a random hug from her father. Looking back, she's sure that these rare exhibits of affection were unintentional – just spontaneous, and involuntary emotional displays of his excitement.

Because their dad was a huge 'boring' sports fan – think curling, golf, and bowling - to gain his attention, Ava and Wendy became boring sports fans too. Both even learned to play those sports, so that they'd have something to talk about with their dad before the next big tournament.

When Ava grew up and clued in that she'd never win her father's affection, nor be exactly who he wanted her to be - she took a 180-degree approach. She packed her bags, moved far, far away from her Ottawa home, experimented with recreational drugs, and went to wild sex parties regularly - that is, until she met her own Mr. Wrong, and fell back into a different kind of useless man cycle.

To this day, the Fischer siblings are close and can laugh at their individual, yet similarly dysfunctional relationships with their father. Wendy chuckles, recounting, *"My dad is so spun, he never visits us, and he certainly has no idea where I live, even though I'm only about a 10-minute drive away. I've invited him over about a thousand times, but he's always somehow busy. And I'm also pretty sure he doesn't know my daughter's name, as he only refers to her as 'the girl.' To make matters worse, he can't follow a conversation at all anymore."* She continued; *"Last weekend, we visited my parents. My dad walked in with a large and expensive selection of fine stinky blue cheeses and scotch (his favourites!), but brought nothing for me, my mom, and my 2 kids. Processed cheese and stale crackers would once again do the trick for us.*

It had been almost 2 months since our last visit, so you'd think he'd be excited to see us. Instead, he smiled and said, 'Hey Wendy, what's new honey?' As I began telling Dad about my new job, home renovations, and the kids' activities, I realized he was engrossed in a golf tournament on TV and hadn't heard one single thing that I'd told him. In mid-sentence I said, 'So I decided to set up a shop on the moon and have tea with the monkeys,' to which he replied, 'That sounds great honey, really great.' Need I say more?"

Ava had a lot more to share about her childhood as it related to her dad, so we met a few times throughout our full interview.

Recalling my own crazy childhood, I asked Ava what her summer holidays were like with her family. She said that they *"were pretty good, especially the annual summer trips to Cape Cod, Massachusetts."*

Ava shared that each summer, she, her siblings Wendy and Tom, and their parents, would spend two glorious sun-soaked weeks with their American relatives in "The Cape." The long, drama-filled road trip to get there, was a whole other story, but the vacation itself was something they excitedly looked forward to.

Every few nights, the families would go out for dinner, to one of the many local seafood places. Given the high cost of lobster in the seafood capital of America, Mr. Fischer would instruct the kids not to order a *"dangerous lobster"* from the menu, because *"although they're dead, their claws are still alive, and they will pinch you."* The kids naturally never (ever) ordered the lobster or any other expensive seafood menu item, but they did respect the bravery of their dad for taking on the near two-pounder at each meal. Today, the much wiser and cultured Ava orders lobster every chance she gets. Not surprisingly, her kids are big fans of the dangerous sea creatures too.

Between leaving his job at the university and opening his own dust-filled, vintage bookstore, Ava's dad decided to try his hand at an in-home law practice. Tasked with having to look after Ava for one day a week (no pre-school on Mondays for two-year-olds, and her mom had to work), her dad would keep Ava locked inside a bathroom outside his large office. He made sure she had plenty of toys, water, and goldfish crackers to last the day.

When his clients would visit and inquire about the strange noises coming from the adjoining restroom, Mr. Fischer would pull a *Wizard of Oz* move and say *"Pay no attention to the noise behind the door"* sort of thing. He played it off as rusty pipes or some other lame, old-home ailment - anything to pretend Ava didn't exist.

Today, Ava and her kids rarely visit her parents. Instead, her mom takes the train from Ottawa to Toronto, to spend the holidays with them. Not surprisingly, her dad is never able to make the trip, but that's okay. Ava says she prefers finally being able to enjoy real attentive family time, and making healthy, happy memories with her mom and kids.

Jackie's Dads

Two heads are better than one, right? How about two dads? My close friend Jackie (Jack) Lehman has an original story, to say the least. I was there when it all unraveled, and I think I was as shocked as Jack, to learn that she was not the biological daughter of Bill Porter – the only dad she'd ever known. And Jack's ancestry was something she had never thought to question, in her nearly forty years on this planet, despite that her features were darker and more exotic than those of her siblings and parents.

On her milestone birthday, Jackie received a Facebook friend request from a man named Enzo Genovese, who claimed that he was her "real," biological father. Poor Jack was stunned. After accepting Dad number 2's (well, really Dad number 1's) Friend request, one of the most bizarre tales of complete craziness unfolded.

Let's start at the beginning...

Jackie and I met by chance when I was running a small interior design business. My beautiful little shop was located on the main street of Port Credit, Ontario, just across the street from Jackie's condo. She told me that when she saw the "Now Open" sign and my ultra-dramatic front window display, she felt instantly drawn to the place. Jackie was a multi-faceted artist who, like me (a writer, marketer, and interior designer), was bursting with creativity and always seeking new outlets to express herself. She was an accomplished florist, live theatre set designer, furniture designer, seamstress, and marketing guru. So, when she entered my shop on a sunny day in early November, we hit it off immediately, and it was a match made in friendship and business partner heaven.

After a 3-hour conversation that felt more like 5 minutes, Jack and I decided to join forces and become a designing duo. "Busy" was the only word to describe our newly branded "Thre3 Design Group (Thre3)." Decorating homes and commercial spaces, pumping out dramatic floral arrangements, designing original acrylic, steel, and reclaimed wood furniture, and creating beautiful modern art, were all in a day's work at Thre3. Keeping up with the demands of our growing clientele was the easy part. Making time for our crazy kids (her 3 and my 3… get it, 'Thre3'), and our mutually controlling and needy husbands - was the real juggle. All things considered, we managed our workloads and personal lives, fairly well.

Days, months, and a creatively stimulating year went by, without incident in our new business - that is, until Jackie learned of her biological dad's existence. After a few days of shock (hers and mine), I decided to probe. Jack rarely discussed her childhood, other than to share that she'd grown up outrageously privileged (raised in a 50 thousand square foot fortress), but she'd also led a very sheltered, and secluded upbringing.

As her story goes, she and her two younger brothers, Aidan, and Ross, were literally hidden away in a (ivory) tower for most of their childhood. Not only were they home-schooled by their neurotic and reclusive mother, Helen, but the location of their home – close to a mountain, deep in the interior of British Columbia, meant that they seldom had outside visitors. Jack's mild-mannered (and brow-beaten) dad, Bill, worked for his father-in-law's successful railcar manufacturing business, and he travelled a lot. This meant that the kids were left alone with their crazy mother for stretches that would last weeks at a time. As I mentioned, Jackie's mom was neurotic, and she became increasingly paranoid as the years went by. The more isolated her little family was kept, the stranger Helen's behaviour towards her children, and the outside world became.

Never mind that the family rarely left the compound, but they even had groceries and household supplies delivered. Jackie remembers walking into her bedroom one afternoon, only to discover that the panes of glass in her large bay window, with an extraordinarily beautiful mountain view (the only perk of her seclusion), had been painted jet black. *"What if someone has binoculars and is spying on you?"* was her mom's justification.

Slowly, incidents like this became the norm, and Jackie and her brothers started to resemble the main characters from *Flowers in the Attic* – an old but very popular series of books, about a mother who starved her children and held them captive in an attic for years. When I was a kid, those books scared the hell out of me.

Whenever Jack's dad returned from one of his lengthy business trips, his wife would reprimand him for spending any time with his kids, as Helen required all his attention. He felt incredibly

22

guilty for being an absent father and husband, so he complied with Helen's every strange request and whim. When Bill was home, Helen was intent on keeping him busy and focused. He was assigned projects like installing iron bars on the main floor windows and extending the height of the palatial homes' gated entrance - all to keep the world out, and their increasingly sheltered children, in.

As the only member of the family who got to experience 'life on the outside,' Bill knew that the family's home life was whacko and that the kids would likely need a lot of therapy when they grew up. That is, if they managed to escape the fortress that was their youth. Bill was also the one family member who could have done something to change their situation – but he lacked self-confidence and clearly, a spine. Instead, he chose to save himself by taking longer and more frequent business trips, as the years passed.

During this troubling time, Jackie's only saving grace was that the compound had acre upon acre of forests, flowers, flowing rivers, and extraordinary trees. She also had her two little brothers who were, sadly, her only companions. Aidan and Ross, six and seven years younger respectively - worshipped their big sis, and they took great delight in spending their afternoons building elaborate tree houses and constructing giant magical creatures from bark, brush, and flowers.

Life, as the incredibly sheltered Porter kids knew it, was for all intents and purposes - pretty good. However, when Jackie reached the age of 18, she got the "itch." Desperately desiring a taste of the outside world, she gathered up all her courage and she grabbed a few clothes, some cash from her mom's "secret drawer" of family dough, and a lone Christmas nutcracker (strangely, she had a collection of thousands). Then... she crossed the moat, hopped the high gate, and headed down the long road to freedom.

When she reached the tiny train station in Golden, British Columbia, Jack bought a one-way ticket to anywhere, Ontario, and she was *"free at last."* Eventually landing in Toronto, she went to the nearest women's shelter, where she recounted her Hansel-and-Gretel-like tale of weird family life, and then she spent the next few months deprogramming and starting to build a life of her own.

In working with a therapist, assigned to her by the women's shelter, Jack was able to understand that her childhood was nothing short of medieval, unnatural, and outright abusive. She learned that her mom was most likely mentally ill, and she had played a sort of "puppet master" role in the family, taking some pleasure from manipulating her husband and children, as well as the environment that they were made to endure.

The fact is, her father never protected Jackie and her brothers, from their inside world. He also never fought (his wife's abuse) to ensure that his kids could experience anything resembling a normal childhood. *"Why?"* was Jackie's big question for so many years. Although she was finally free from *Mommy Dearest* and *Daddy Do-Nothing*, she still needed to know why she had led such a sheltered childhood, and why her dad did nothing to fix the situation.

More than 20 years later, Jackie finally learned the truth from her new Facebook friend "father." In short, her conception was a secret, that needed to be kept concealed. In her mother's deteriorating mind, she wanted to do everything in her power to keep Jackie safe, and "hidden" from the truth.

You see, Jackie's mom came from a very wealthy manufacturing family. They designed and mass-produced railway cars for freight trains, to supply North American railway systems. As a teen, Jackie's mom was rebellious and wild. She hated conformity, and she railed against her parent's conservative and strict ways. Despite Helen's nature, her parents had made very clear plans for her future, which included marrying the son of an equally wealthy and impressive family. That son was Jackie's dad, Bill Porter. However, everything changed one night, when Helen attended a house party. She hooked up with an equally wild Italian boy named Enzo, and she got herself 'knocked up.'

To keep the identity of the baby's true father under wraps, Helen's parents along with Bill's parents, quickly married "the kids," so that Jackie could be raised as Bill's own daughter. Enzo, whom the families regarded as *"The kid from the other side of the tracks,"* was given an all-expenses-paid trip to Europe and $10,000 cash to buzz off, which is just what the young opportunist did.

Some 40 years later, the newly born-again-Christian, Enzo, decided it was time to come clean, if he was going to make it through the pearly gates with a spotless record. Cleansing his soul and his conscience meant putting the burden on his unsuspecting offspring, Jackie. And with that, the useless man "Friended" and became Dad #2 to my friend, "Jackie Porter-Lehman-Genovese."

Deadbeat Duds

Sometimes, men who have children, like to pretend that they don't have children. This usually happens after a divorce. The husband leaves the wife (or the wife leaves the husband), and the kids somehow get left in the dust by their deadbeat dads. I recently started watching old episodes of Shameless, a dramedy that centers on siblings in a (very) dysfunctional Chicago family, who struggle to survive adolescence, while coping with their alcoholic father.

With their mother out of the picture (she's also a total deadbeat, for the record), the eldest daughter, Fiona, has been forced to take care of her father, Frank and her five younger siblings. Frank is the ultimate deadbeat dad. He has no care in the world, other than for when his next disability cheque will be arriving, so that he can cash it in and spend it on important things like booze, booze, and more booze. The show is hilarious, however, the horrific parental neglect by this character, and the subsequent damage he causes his children, is no laughing matter.

Unfortunately, I know a few men who reside in "Deadbeat Dad Land," and another one who is inching his way into that territory. Theirs are not funny stories, especially for the children they've left behind. These tales are tragic and depressing, and just plain sh*tty. For this reason, I've decided to skip my own tragic deadbeat dud tales and have opted to borrow some material from a great writer named Heather O'Neill, a contributor to *The Walrus*, an independent, non-profit Canadian media organization.

In O'Neill's article, *On Deadbeat Dads*, she shares her thoughts on the gifts, the gall and the grief surrounding deadbeat dads:

"There's a holiday in late December that I call Deadbeat Dad Week. It falls a week after Christmas because that's when gifts from absentee fathers show up in the mail. Deadbeat Dads send their parcels on December 24. They never have any idea what their kids want for Christmas. They just buy the most nifty, outrageous thing they come across.

When I was eight, in Montreal during the 1980s, my friend Stuart was sent a Great Dane puppy and needed a paper route to afford the dog food. Marie received a strobe light for the ceiling of her bedroom. Ted opened an enormous box and discovered a foot-wide tennis ball. Jean-Phillippe got the best gift: a megaphone. He stood outside repeating, "Step away from your vehicle," to people getting into their cars.

Deadbeat Dad typically wears sunglasses and leather jackets. He has long hair, even though he's balding on top. He rides a skateboard at age thirty-five. He's fit and is often spotted in the playground doing chin-ups on the monkey bars. When children are with Deadbeat Dad, they always feel in the flush of a new relationship. Everything Deadbeat Dad says is a riot. He does the most exciting things. He wrestles snakes! He eats shark! He runs into Ozzy Osbourne in bars!

Deadbeat Dad never has a steady paycheque. His excuses for this are epic, and should be published in pocket-sized form, just like those books of quotations from Oscar Wilde. Deadbeat Dad always claims that money is coming. He says he plans to open a massage parlour in the garage. He's awaiting a court settlement from being bitten by a German shepherd in Detroit. He bought a painting at a yard sale that he's sure is worth a bundle.

Deadbeat Dad thinks he has a calling. He has shoeboxes filled with demo tapes he recorded in his bathroom, where "the acoustics are awesome." He has notebooks filled with ballpoint pen drawings of horses. He writes poetry on the back of paper placemats.

Deadbeat Dad likes to remind his children that they exist because of his marvellous genes. Thanks to them, his kids are good in sports, ace spelling bees, and land their first jobs at Dunkin' Donuts. Deadbeat Dad acts as if his genes are the magic beans his children's mother traded her future for.

Deadbeat Dad is always a little depressed. After all, he has time on his hands to wallow in self-pity. He'd never have time for existential dilemmas if he were actually raising his kids.

Deadbeat Dad gets arrested for possessing unlicensed firearms or disturbing the peace. He has issues with drugs and alcohol. He is a good time, with his video arcades, roller coasters, and Whack-a-Moles, but he is a stranger to his children. He doesn't know their favourite books. He doesn't know the name of the bully who teased his son in grade four. He doesn't take his daughter out for dinner after she stars in her school play. He disappears for long stretches, during which children grow up.

Once his children are grown, Deadbeat Dad might come back to make amends. He wants to be close to his kids, like other parents. To this end, he uses "the apology." Apologies are like flowers that bloom on the side of a cactus. They're startling and lovely. Sadly, though, they are not time machines, and Deadbeat Dad cannot use them to travel back and show up at your eighth birthday party.

My daughter went to meet her biological father last year, just after Christmas. He said he wanted to give her presents to her in person. She hadn't seen him since she was five. Back then, he'd disappear on week-long benders. He'd show up high as a kite to take her to the park. He'd entertain her with handstands and juggling and then fall asleep on a bench.

He stole my clothes and schoolbooks. He stole my television, guitar, and radio. I'd pass the pawnshop and see half my apartment for sale in the window. He never paid a penny of child support, and after years of begging and taking him to court, I gave up. Ten years went by, and my daughter and I almost forgot he existed. He never came up in conversation. We were reminded of him only when the presents arrived at Christmas and on her birthday. They were good gifts: iPods, cameras, and other things I couldn't afford.

My daughter wanted to meet him, and I couldn't dissuade her. She brought her dog along, full of expectations. She was taken aback from the get-go. His front tooth was broken in half. He had a new girlfriend with him, who sat silently observing them. Circling his arm was a tattoo of a squid, which he claimed was his favourite animal. He was working as a bicycle courier and was still broke.

I asked her if she found that her dad looked like her.

'My God, yes. It was shocking! All the missing features!'

'Will you see him again? '

'No' she said. 'He made me feel weird. I almost wish I'd never met him. Why didn't you stop me? '

One of the burdens of single motherhood is letting children figure out the truth about Deadbeat Dads on their own. Maybe it's for the best that my daughter writes her father off. Deadbeat Dads can never give you anything but shiny baubles and disappearing acts. It never pays to love them. One thing that's true about all Deadbeat Dads is that they'll break your heart.

2

SOMETIMES YOU'VE GOT TO KISS A FEW FROGS

*"It's better to be healthy alone, than sick
with someone else." – Dr. Phil McGraw*

My early dating years were lots of fun - young love, and all that stuff. That's not to say that the emotional trials and tribulations of having boyfriends didn't take their toll on my young and unjaded heart. For every prince, there were many frogs to kiss.

First, there was Frank. He was a few years older, and with his broad shoulders and smouldering, big brown eyes, every girl in my high school, nearly tripped over herself to get close to him. Not only was he a total babe, but he was also super charming, and for some strange reason, he liked me. At the ripe old age of 16, that guy was ultra-smooth with the ladies. He was a macho Italian boy, who had the "cajones" to ask my macho Italian dad, if he could take me on a date, before actually asking me out.

Soon into our boyfriend-girlfriend status, Frank took me for dinner at his aunt and uncle's popular pizza restaurant. We then had plans to go to a movie before he'd promised to drop me home, to make my 11 p.m. curfew. After the delicious (free) meal at the family restaurant, Frank grabbed me by the hand, led me to his car, and literally threw me into the front seat of his Camaro. I thought to myself, "At *least he opened the door for me*." On the way to the movie theatre, he persuaded me to take a little detour with him so that we could *"look at the amazing stars."* As he drove down the unlit and unpaved road, I had sirens going off in my head. I remembered my father's loving words of advice, and I instantly felt panicked; *"Don't smoke, don't do drugs, and for God's sake, don't get pregnant. If you can live by those three rules, you'll be okay, kid."*

As Frank pulled into a grassy parking lot and turned off the engine, he confidently slipped his hand up the front of my t-shirt, and his tongue down my throat - as my father's three *"don'ts"* rang loudly in my ears. Naturally, I fought him off – hard. When he wouldn't budge, I threatened to tell his mother that he forced himself on me. Frank feared no one except his mother – who was apparently a skilled warrior with a wooden spoon. With terror in his eyes, Frank instantly retreated, and his parting words to me, as he pushed me out the passenger's side door, and onto the grass, were *"Be sure to tell your daddy he doesn't have to worry about anyone knocking you up, prude!"*

Boys in Men's Clothing

There is nothing so strange and wonderful as the high school prom. It doesn't matter how long (or short) ago it was, but this major milestone event has always been a rite of passage for teen boys and girls. Boys are awkward in their man suits, and girls are uncomfortably squeezed into tight dresses and heels, like pageant queens. Prom night is often the first time that curfews and skirts are lifted, and boyfriends and girlfriends "go all the way."

How many boys (and girls) have lost their virginity at the high school prom? We rarely remember the second person we had sex with, but our first? Always. I remember it like it was yesterday. Every single second leading up to the big, and let's face it, non-event, is as vivid as a glorious pink and purple sunset. We will never forget our first, whether it's true love, puppy love, or just a "get 'er done" kind of love. Our first time can never be relived, nor can our high school prom.

I recently read my friend Pete's novella, "*Splooge*", a month-by-month account of his coming-of-age story... As an aside, I've realized that I'm a sh*tty writer in comparison to Pete. Boy can that man paint a picture with words. In his story, Pete recounts losing his virginity to "Janet" at his high school prom. It was as awkward to read about, as I'm sure the event was in real life.

Like Pete, I lost "it" to "Jim" after my senior prom. Jim was nice, simple, and easy-going. He was a quality guy, who used to complete my math and history homework. While our mutual first time was predictably uncomfortable and anything but mind-blowing, it was still, minute-by-minute, memorable.

My entire family still fondly remembers (and often reminisces about) the time leading up to my short-lived relationship with Jim, as "*The Rob years.*" At the ripe old age of 16, Rob was a six foot four, V-backed Adonis in a Quicksilver t-shirt and flowered surfer shorts. However, his physical perfection paled, in comparison to his big, beautiful, and bold personality. His greatest asset, however, was his innocent nature. He was clueless that his appearance and mere presence drove all teenage girls wild. And this made him truly loveable.

I met Rob (Robby) Barnes when we were in elementary school - he was in the sixth grade, and I was in the fifth. Rob and his younger brother Ricky had recently moved to my hometown, from Bum Fuck Nowhere, Northern Ontario, with their recently single (and gorgeous) mom, Marion. The boys were nice guys - so adorably cute, too. Rob was tiny – just four foot eight at the time. By contrast, his just one-year younger brother, was already five foot seven, and he was in my class.

Ricky was yummy. With his dirty blond hair and smoky brown eyes, he was the spitting image of a young Patrick Swayze. I, and the rest of the fifth-grade geek squad, only had eyes for Ricky. And I felt like I was slowly making progress with him too. By the beginning of seventh grade, Ricky was dropping by my house regularly after dinner to ask me out on bike ride "dates." I was so smitten. I knew that by the end of that year, Ricky and I would be going out – whatever that looked like at our age.

Then the unthinkable happened. My parents announced that they'd be pulling me out of my school at Christmas time because we were moving across town. To make matters worse, they enrolled me in a very strict Catholic school, where my awkward and skinny, five-foot-ten-inch frame, was aggressively recruited for every sports team, by the school's head athletic coach. Mr. McAleer tried to convince me that my height and wiry frame were perfect for all sports, despite that other than long-distance running on my own, I felt I had no athletic ability. He didn't care though. Mr. McAleer was like a lion on an antelope, and he was determined to make an athletic superstar out of me, whether I believed in myself or not.

At my new school, I very quickly became a different girl. I learned to dribble a ball (and quite proficiently get it in a basket), and I was taught how to high jump, and to win every long-distance race in my age group. Under Mr. McAleer's supervision, I became a well-rounded athletic star. In fact, I was so into sports and winning, that I completely forgot about boys until I went to high school.

Grade nine was scary. I was no longer known as the queen of the basketball court and the running track. I was just a small number, at a giant high school, and as a "minor niner," I had no choice but to take my rightful place at the bottom of the status barrel. The only thing I had to look forward to was trying out for the basketball team. I easily made the team and, was quickly promoted to the senior team, three years ahead of my age. On the day of the regional championship game, I was in fine form. I scored the winning basket (and the twelve before that), and my teammates carried me out of the gym on their shoulders.

After a quick shower, I did my hair and make-up, and I put on a powder-pink dress, that my dad had bought me on one of his work trips to New York. As I was waiting outside the stadium for my parents to take me to my victory dinner, I remember feeling proud of myself, and truly pretty for the first time in my life. Deep in self-indulgent thought, I was taken aback by a *"Hey there"* from a God-like creature, who was standing behind me. As I turned, my heart skipped a beat. It was the boy of my dreams - literally. I'd never seen him before, and short of being Jake Ryan, from my favourite teen coming-of-age movie, *Sixteen Candles*, this guy had everything that any 15-year-old girl could ever possibly dream of getting close to. My embarrassing response was, *"Hay is for horses."* He ignored my sassiness and continued, *"Aren't you Ellie Russo?"* Literally, too stunned to answer my dream boy truthfully, (because he actually knew my name), my immediate (and again embarrassing) response was, *"No, I'm Jane Doe."*

Suddenly, my ride appeared, thank God, and I hopped in before my legs gave way to my first real and most extraordinary crush on Robby Barnes. That was the same formerly four-foot-eight cutie pie, Robby Barnes, from Bum Fuck Nowhere Northern Ontario, and my old elementary school.

Later that night, my mother took a call on our home phone (this was before cell phones). Upon hanging up, she announced to me, my dad, and my three siblings, that I would be going on a movie date the following Friday with Marion Barnes's boy, Rob. I nearly died ... of embarrassment, shock, fear, and pure excitement. I was totally sleepless that night, knowing that my upcoming Friday night movie date, which my mother of all people, had arranged, was the best thing that would ever happen to me, in my 15 years on the planet.

Yadda, yadda, yadda. With Robby, I had my first real date, my first real kiss, and two and a half years of being the girlfriend of the most popular boy in town. Those years were glorious. I truly loved Robby, and not in the 'puppy' sense. Then came Rob's prom. He went to a different high school, and he was a year older, so when he asked me to his senior prom, I was excited to embark on the most romantic milestone event of our young lives, with my one true love.

That is, until the prom and the after-party ended, and we entered the hotel room Robby had booked for our special "first" night together. I'd like to say that this was one of those magical, and rarely beautiful loss of mutual virginity stories - but it wasn't. It was a disaster. I wanted to, but I just couldn't do it. I wasn't ready (for some insane reason), and he dumped me on the spot. Apparently "blue balls" is a real and serious ailment for young men to suffer, so he needed to leave me, and find his cure. Naturally, I had to accept his decision (and the guilt that went with mine to remain a virgin), but still, I was devastated.

Three weeks later, without a word from my beloved, when I was finally getting my appetite back, and feeling like my crumbled world was starting to piece itself together, the inevitable happened. Robby showed up at my high school, and he was there to visit "Niki," a senior whose locker was just three down from mine. Predictably, Robby lost his virginity to ultra-experienced Niki, and I gave mine away in "get er' done" fashion, to Jim. Happily-never after was in the cards for Robby and me... a useless mistake, I sometimes still regret.

Heeeeere's Johnny

Between the ages of 18 and 20, boys came and went - some good, some bad, but Johnny took the cake. It was the summer between my first and second year of university when we first met, and I was officially a woman. I could go to bars without having to peddle my fake ID, and I looked womanly enough to attract the attention of older men. Johnny saw me as an easy target. One night at a dance club in downtown Toronto, 23-year-old Johnny, sauntered up to me and handed me a vodka ginger ale, with a twist of lime. He'd clearly been watching me, and he knew my drink. I was so impressed. He was confident, and he was gorgeous. He was 6'2, had thick and wavy dark brown hair, a cleft chin, and crystal blue eyes. I was instantly in love, and under his spell.

We quickly became a legitimate couple, albeit a long-distance one. I spent the next three years taking trains from London, Ontario, where I lived and attended university as an English Literature major, to Toronto, where he lived, and worked as a pharmaceutical salesman. Although Johnny, who owned a car, rarely made the trip the two hours west of his city to visit me, I still managed to see him almost every weekend.

When I arrived each Friday night in Toronto, by what felt like a cattle car, Johnny was rarely at the train station to greet me, so I'd schlep my big overnight bag on the streetcar, to his condo in the west end of the city. Before entering his place with the key he'd graciously cut for me, I stopped by the 24-hour market near his place, to grab some groceries. Johnny never had food in his fridge, but he sure loved a home-cooked meal, and I was always happy to oblige. Lucky for Johnny, and thanks to my dysfunctional childhood, I'd been honing my culinary skills since I was 12.

Weekend in and out, this routine went on for the entire 3 years we were together. I'd get myself to Johnny's place, then spend the whole weekend cooking, cleaning, and fawning over my older handsome man - just the way he liked it. He rarely took me out on the town, selling me on the idea that being a homebody was the most attractive quality for someone who could be his future wife. When the weekend was done, he'd drop me back at the train station – usually early Sunday afternoon, because he needed the rest of the day to "decompress" before his busy work week ahead.

Eventually, doting on Johnny, which was once a labour of love, started to feel like just plain labour. In the last year of our relationship, more often than not, I'd arrive at Johnny's place around dinner time, only to have him call and apologize, because he needed to work late, or he was obligated to go for drinks with a client. Thoughtfully, he always asked me to keep dinner warm for him and *"not to wait up."* Not surprisingly, it turned out that the working late thing was merely a cover-up for an affair that he was having with a busty blonde named Tammy.

One Friday night, I was determined to not sit home alone again, so I got dressed up and ventured out into the big, scary city by myself. After eating alone in a nice little pasta place on College Street, where my tears practically turned my shrimp fettuccine into bouillabaisse, I left the restaurant and headed towards Johnny's place, on foot.

As I walked along College Street, I saw them. Johnny and Tammy were leaving a surprisingly seedy bar together, and his hand was around her waist, with his fingers tucked inside the back of her (too) short skirt's waistband. There was no confusing Pam Anderson's even bustier and certainly dumber carbon copy, for a client or a colleague.

I think the sting of that moment will live with me forever. Like a deer in headlights, I was frozen - unable to confront him. Instead, I hailed a cab back to Johnny's place and packed my things. The pasta with cream sauce I had prepared for him, still sat on the counter covered in foil. Before I left his place for the last time, I made sure to crush up a strong cocktail of killer laxatives - that I found in his well-stocked medicine cabinet. I mixed it into *"Dear John's"* dinner and caught the last train to Clarksville, so to speak. I never heard from Johnny again. He knew that I knew what he was up to, and he also knew better than to ever reach out again.

I'd like to say that I never laid eyes on the schmuck again, but that all changed about 4 years ago. For my friend's 45th birthday, we decided to take a girls' weekend trip to the city that never sleeps. Four women were booked to go, but only two of us showed up at the little island airport in downtown Toronto, early on the Thursday morning that we were to depart for NYC. It was no big deal though. The birthday girl and I would still go and share a luxury suite for four at the trendy downtown ACE hotel in Manhattan for three nights, and four glorious days of kid-less recklessness. The other two women (and moms) had been roped into kid-related obligations, and they begrudgingly gave up their plane seats and comfy beds in our suite.

Being the (truly) horrible flyer that I am, I was terrified to learn that Kiki (the birthday girl) and I could not sit next to each other on the flight. Whose hand would I claw as the plane ascended and descended? Well, wouldn't you know who sat next to me? Johnny. That's right, Tammy-lusting Johnny, that I had left poisoned all those years ago.

As the now silver-haired fox sat next to me, my old life flashed before my eyes. *"Could it really be him, and could this really be happening?"* I thought. As he turned to me with a polite *"Hello,"* I realized that he was the same shallow douchebag that I'd dated so many years before. I have to say, I looked awesome. I was a little thinner than I was back then, and I had changed my hair colour from brown to blond. I'd also found my confidence and total intolerance for useless men. When I replied, *"Hi Johnny,"* he looked at me with confusion, and said very innocently, *"Forgive me, but do we know each other?"* I said, *"Yes, Johnny, we sure do. In fact, we used to date, quite seriously, for 3 years. But that was many years ago. It's Ellie."* His reply was enthusiastic and hopeful. *"Oh my God, Ellie, of course. If I'd known you'd be looking so smoking at this age, I'd have never treated you so badly,"* and then he laughed that incredibly annoying laugh that I suddenly remembered.

It was only 8:15 a.m., but I quickly flagged the flight attendant for a glass of shitty white airplane wine, then gulped it down. If I was going to be trapped beside this guy for over an hour, I'd make the most of my precious time. A little liquid courage couldn't hurt either. I decided to take Johnny on, telling him how his poor treatment of me had impacted me for many years after I left him. I also told him that he'd be sorry when my book came out. He loved it. In true narcissistic form, he laughed and laughed as I spilled my tongue-in-cheek guts, while I downed another glass of wine. He also decided that while he had me trapped, he'd try to impress me with pictures of the Ferrari, fancy cottage, and palatial home, that he once shared with his ex, "Tammy." I made sure to let him know how unimpressive he still was, and that he did me a favour by showing me his true colours, decades ago.

We innocently sparred until we landed. As we exited the aircraft, I grabbed Kiki and said, *"Let's make a break for it."* She was a real trooper. With three glasses of wine to my two, she courageously said, *"No, let the jerk pay for the ride to our hotel,"* which is exactly what he did. Before exiting the limo that he had waiting for him at LaGuardia airport, we exchanged numbers. I'm not sure why I gave him mine or took his, but it somehow felt like payback to give him false hope. He's been texting me ever since. I have yet to reply. Now that's closure - real closure. There's no cure for a truly useless man, like hitting the red "decline" button on your phone.

3

HUSBAND NUMBER ONE – FATHER OF MY FIRST TWO

"I married beneath me - all women do."
- Nancy Astor, in a speech in Oldham, England, 1951

The best years of my life were wasted on Hubby Number 1. Other than leaving me with high anxiety and crippling debt, he did manage to facilitate two of my greatest joys in life, Julia, and Andrew. Greg, or "Teffy," as his friends called him because he was like Teflon, in that nothing stuck to him, was the epitome of a control freak.

Even though we met at work, and I was his employee, we were both single and in our 20s, so there was no salacious scandal. And I was certain that he would be my knight in shining armour. He had everything a wide-eyed girl in search of a fine husband and life-long stability, was looking for. He had a great career, a loving family, fun friends, and a very strong sense of self. Most of it was good, except for that strong sense of self thing.

Teffy, as I'll call him from here on, for fear of a certain slander lawsuit, was scary, but not in the traditional sense. He was meticulous - think Julia Roberts' husband in the thriller, *Sleeping with the Enemy*. He had dough, which meant he had a nice condo, nice cars - yes, cars - and a fat bank account. That's not to say that his income (combined with mine) afforded us a lot of extras, though.

When we were married and had kids, his approach to spending became *"Why waste good money on things like kids' toys or*

41

essential household items, when one expensive sofa and an HDTV would do the trick?" The wine cellar, though – now that was his real baby. Man-oh-man could that man spend money and boundless time and energy on building the perfect collection. Every third Saturday of the month was "Wine Release Saturday," which in his world meant, *"Listen, babe, if you happen to go into labour with our first kid on a Friday, you'd better make it early because you know I need to spend my whole Saturday purchasing wine and managing my collection."*

In the two months leading up to the birth of our first child, I reduced my work schedule to four days a week, as I'd been experiencing some severe pregnancy-related sciatic nerve issues. This meant (in Teffy's mind) that I would have one whole extra day a week, in addition to the entire weekend, to work on household projects, before the baby came. On my first Friday morning "off" from work, I woke to find a giant list entitled "Home Summer Projects" on our kitchen table. Teffy had thoughtfully left this list for me to work my way through, over the next few months, until the baby came. The list included simple tasks like:

- *Replace faucet in kitchen*
- *Clean all baseboards in house*
- *Paint front woodwork*
- *Replace flower bed in front of house*
- *Paint iron railing in front of house*
- *Etc., etc.*

When I found the list, I was waiting for Teffy to pop around the corner laughing at the hilarity of his prank. Sadly, there was nothing funny about the giant "To-do" list, except the additional bullets, my friends added when they discovered the page that had now been moved to the fridge door by Teffy. Their additions were priceless, and kept me laughing when I should have been crying:

- *Repair potholes on Adelaide Street*
- *Begin construction on Hwy 407*

Hooray – It's Wine Release Saturday!

Remember what I said about Teffy's request for me to give birth on Friday, so as not to interfere with his wine purchasing plans? Well, wouldn't you know it, our little darling Julia was born at 10:44 p.m. on a Friday evening. Don't get me wrong, Teffy stayed for the birth (just barely), but he needed to get home and get his rest before the big wine release lineup started at 7 a.m. the next morning. Long story short: our first child went three days without a name because Teffy had his wine buying and cataloguing priorities.

When I think about the first few weeks of my first baby's life, I'll never forget that incredible exhaustion. What I wouldn't have given for a few hours of solid sleep. After seven straight days of nursing on demand, all day, and all night, I caved and begged my husband for a little relief. After feeding Julia at 3 a.m., I asked if he'd mind taking the baby for a few hours so that I could get some lifesaving (mine and the baby's) sleep. It was Friday night (technically Saturday), so Teffy didn't need to get up for work the next morning, and thankfully there wasn't a wine release that weekend. In my delirium, I rationalized that I wasn't asking too much of him - she was his kid, too, after all, right? Wrong.

Do you know what that guy did? He stood over me with the baby as I slept, holding her as uncomfortably as he possibly could, while she wailed at the top of her little lungs. His plan worked. As soon as I had laid my head on the pillow, I was up again, in full care-for-baby-at-all-cost mode. Crying, I carefully crawled down the stairs to the TV room, doing my best not to interrupt my husband's precious sleep.

Fast forward to when Julia was five months old, and the house and I by that time, were well-oiled machines. I had gone back to work early, full-time, as a communications manager for a big Fortune 500 company, and we had a live-in nanny who was rarely seen outside of working hours. I still managed to race home during my lunch hour to breastfeed (then back to work), and then I was back home by 5:15 p.m., getting a lovely home-cooked meal ready and on the table for Teffy by 6:00 p.m. sharp, when he walked in.

Don't get me wrong, Teffy was always thankful and courteous about the effort I put into meals. The crumbs falling to the floor from Julia's highchair, however, drove him crazy. He couldn't stand it. He hated anything that was out of place. In this "perfect" first marriage, I often felt like a case study from a 1960s high school home economics manual:

"To be a proper wife:

Have dinner ready. Plan ahead, even the night before, to have a delicious meal ready on time for your husband's return from work. This is a way of letting him know that you have been thinking about him and are concerned about his needs...

Prepare yourself. Take 15 minutes to rest so you will be refreshed when he arrives. Touch up your make-up, put a ribbon in your hair and be fresh looking. He has just been with a lot of work weary people. Be a little gay and a little more interesting

for him. His boring day may need a lift and one of your duties
is to provide it."

Be a little gay? Are you kidding me? God, what I wouldn't have given at that point - with a new kid, demanding job, and a control freak husband, to spend some leisurely time shopping or having lunch with my best, gay friend, Jamie!

"Clear away the clutter, gather up schoolbooks, toys, papers, etc. and then run a dust cloth over the tables. During the colder months of the year, you should prepare and light a fire for him to unwind by. Your husband will feel he has reached a haven of rest and order and it will give you a lift too. After all, catering for his comfort will provide you with immense personal satisfaction. Minimize all noise . . . encourage the children to be quiet . . . remember his topics of conversation are more important than yours."

Clearly, my husband took a serious page (or two) from that book. And so went my marriage with Teffy, a real Ward Cleaver on crack type. All was perfect in my exhausting world as long as I played June to his Ward, and until the fateful day when our daughter Julia got the runs on the sisal rug in his office, and the family home was soiled forever.

A few years later, Andrew was born. Upon entering the hospital to give birth, Teffy said, *"You don't seem to be in too much pain. Maybe we can get you checked in, and then we can go catch a flick. It's such a beautiful day – let's not waste it."* The movie never happened, as Andrew came into the world just a few hours later, on a Saturday afternoon. Again, Teffy didn't miss one minute of work, even though he was the President of his company by that time.

I'd learned my lesson the last time around, and I went straight from the hospital to my mother's home, two hours away, for almost three weeks. In that time, Teffy got lots of new parent rest, and my mother helped me with my kids, and she saved my life from exhaustion and my husband's demanding ways. To this day, it was the best non-vacation I've ever had.

4

HUSBAND NUMBER TWO – THE MISTAKE ON THE TAKE

"The best gift a man ever gave me was a divorce!"
- Author unknown

Surprise, surprise – "Ward and June" didn't make it. It wasn't the 60s anymore, after all, and I just got too damned tired of trying to keep up with the impossible schedule. So, I left. Teffy fought me (hard) in court and spent a big whack of cash on the most vicious legal divorce team he could find. It nearly wiped me out, but the money I had to spend to get that little piece of paper, was worth the cost of my freedom.

Naturally, I stayed in the suburbs where my kids attended school, and Teffy bought himself a pristine, 3-bedroom condo that housed minimal furniture, and very few toys. It was okay though, the kids only had to be there every second weekend, and their dad opted to take them out on "his days" (in other words, "keep them out"), rather than have to deal with their mess in his pristine home, with only him to clean it.

The freedom I gained was an awakening – albeit, short-lived. I suddenly had every second weekend away from the kids, and a lot of time to myself. I went to the movies on Saturday afternoons, had kid-less lunches with my friends, and I even went out dancing once in a while. The break from being a 24/7/365 caregiver and servant brought me greater joy and fulfilment. It also made me a much better mom, and the kids sensed it. At my house, Julia and Andrew got to make a mess and lots of regular kid mistakes. We baked and made crafts together, and sometimes we left the evidence on the counters and the floors until the next day. Cleaning and being perfect all the time was no longer the end game. And the end result was some much-needed fun in our lives. The kids loved being with far-from-perfect me, and they seemed relieved to have found their own sense of freedom in this new parenting arrangement.

Foolishly, about 2 years into my new-found free rein, I made a tragic mistake and fell for a boy-man. You see, Derek was a man only in looks. He was a Daddy's boy, and a beer-drinking, sports-watching guys-guy, who also had a penchant for full-blown temper tantrums. This behaviour wasn't something new or reserved for the woman in his life. It seemed to have been there from the beginning, and it was somehow his birthright. I say this because I witnessed a few of these tantrums in the presence of his mother, his female cousins, and his aunts. All of them put up the behaviour as though they were witnessing a 2-year-old throwing a fit. They just accepted it, and moved on, without paying him any attention.

By deciding to accept this deplorable behaviour for myself, I guess I deserved what was coming to me. Hadn't I learned anything? I knew better, but I didn't listen to that no-so-little voice in my head, telling me to run like the wind. As to why I fell for the boy-man? That was simple. He was a hunk, and he seemed slightly exotic to me. His parents were from Warsaw, Poland, and he was worldly and "old-fashioned," which I mistook for being chivalrous. He had beautiful green eyes (slightly beady, mind you), an incredible body, and an incredible sense of confidence that made you trust him and feel safe. What more could a girl want? "*A lot*" is the only answer to this question. I guess I was infatuated with Derek, but I was also totally stupid.

This guy didn't cook. He didn't clean. And the biggest red flag - he made the chick (aka "Moi") pick up the tab for evenings out, more times than I can cringingly remember. While all of this was clearly a recipe for disaster from the get-go, I'd been well-trained in my last relationships (including with my father), to win the man over at all costs. I was also very attracted to him, and I liked the passion I felt with this challenging specimen. Because his mother, whom I really adored, put up with his ridiculous behaviour seemingly unscathed, she sort of drilled it into my head that this is what it was like being married to an Eastern European man, so I should just get used to it. I tried – oh how I tried.

Every day with Derek meant doing the cooking, the cleaning, and basically doting on the dud twenty ways to Sunday. After three long years of this nonsense, I finally got wise. My kids knocked some sense into me too, by convincing me I was worth more, so I broke up with my useless boyfriend. Once more I was free, *"free at last!"* - and I toasted with my best girlfriends, who started to see the light in me, that had dimmed while I was in a relationship with Derek.

For the next two months, life was truly grand. I spent quality and tension-free time with my kids, I went out on girls' nights, and I even purchased a new house. *"A fresh start,"* I told myself. Though I'd never actually lived with the man-child, he had spent a lot of time in my home being catered to, and I spent a lot of my free time prettying up his ugly bachelor pad in the city.

Once I was finally where I wanted to be in my life, I suffered *"The scream that could be heard around the world"* (as my brother now calls it), early one Saturday morning. My kids were with my ex, and my brother Jay and his wife Tracey were spending the weekend. The night before, we enjoyed a nice dinner, a few glasses of wine, and wound down the evening with a funny movie (*Napoleon Dynamite* to be exact). I woke up the next morning before they did, hoping to get a jump on the day. I had just purchased a new home, so I needed to pack up the one I was in. I decided to start with my bedroom's en-suite bathroom. Being decidedly efficient, I was going to pack as little as possible, knowing full well that most things would be boxed up, and just collecting dust in the garage of my new home.

When I saw the pregnancy test box at the bottom of a bathroom drawer, I literally looked up and gave a little *"Thank you"* to the good Lord above, that I would never need one of these again. *"What the heck,"* I thought, *"Pee on the damn stick and throw it away. It would be one less thing to move, and those tests are a small fortune. It's best not to 'waste' it."*

Having been on the pill for years and knowing my child-bearing years were behind me, I didn't give it another thought as I threw the soiled test in the trash, without checking the result. Later that morning, once I'd packed up my entire bedroom, I decided I'd do an illegal garbage dump run with my SUV, to the big commercial trash bin behind the local Tim Horton's. As I went to grab the garbage from the bathroom, "Surprise!!!" - the two lines confirming my pregnancy practically jumped out of the trash can and knocked me on the floor. I was pregnant. Holy shit—I was f*%#ing pregnant! I screamed, and I screamed, and I screamed and . . . you get the point.

My sister-in-law got to me first. Tracey had one finger on the speed dial of her cell phone, assuming I'd lost a limb, and she needed to call 911. My brother, in typical useless man fashion, just rolled over in bed - that is, until I shook him awake, crying like the hysterical woman that I was at that moment.

Having been born with a typically unhealthy dose of Catholic guilt, abortion was not an option for me. However, if God had seen fit to bring me a miscarriage, I'd have happily taken it. Looking back now, I can't imagine life without my little Ella, "Ba-Goo." As a baby, she was practically perfect, except for the extreme temper tantrums she threw regularly. But it's not her fault, she had to inherit something from her man-child father. I take solace in knowing that when Ella is a grown-up, she'll be okay, just as long as she never learns to cook or clean, and she forgets her wallet when she goes on dinner dates.

After sitting on the big news for a few days, unable to drown my sorrows in booze like I usually would have, I called the jerk and let him in on the pending birth of his only child. He was thrilled and strutting like a peacock. I could practically feel the overabundance of testosterone over the phone, while he "mansplained" to me that his super sperm was more potent than regular men's, so naturally they *"pulverized"* (his word not mine) the 99.99% effectiveness of my (useless) birth control pills.

There's not much more to say about this situation, other than the Derek period in my life, was unfortunate. Once I accepted the fact that we were having a baby together, the inevitable happened. We got back together, we had the kid, we moved in together, we got married, and all was as expected – life was perfectly crappy! It's worth noting that when Derek moved into my home and contributed next to nothing, his newly renovated (by me), 2-bedroom condo was being rented out for a pretty penny, and I certainly didn't see any of those proceeds.

Less than a year into this second marriage, my older kids helped me "*step into the light*" once again, and we escaped the wrath of the con artist. My second divorce cost me a bundle in legal fees (once again), and I had to pay him a big portion from the sale of my (the "marital") home. Derek, of course, scored - he got to keep his old bachelor pad in the city, and he bought himself a shiny new condo and a BMW, with the proceeds from the sale of my home. It turns out he's got himself a new woman, too. I wish her all the best.

5

OTHER WOMEN'S HUSBANDS

"If you want things said, ask a man. If you want things done, ask a woman." - Margaret Thatcher

Liz's Procrastinator

My friend Liz's husband is a successful master carpenter. Emmanuel (Manny) works mostly on residential projects like new, ultra-high-end subdivisions, and he manages everything from framing homes to installing gorgeous, coffered mahogany ceilings and crown mouldings. The homes Manny builds are nothing short of magnificent.

His own home, by major contrast, was in terrible disrepair until recently. The roof was sagging, the kids had put holes in the walls, and the hardwood was literally bubbling from a leak that happened more than a year ago. Aside from the things that needed to be fixed around the house, there were Manny's "projects" to be dealt with. There was a solarium that was roughed in two years ago, then abandoned. The new hardwood floors, and the extra bedroom project in the basement, became a deathtrap for Liz's two kids, and miniature pinscher, so the entire area had been rendered *"off limits,"* until Manny could eventually get to it. These are just two of the many examples of the renovations that got started, but never completed.

A few weeks ago, I met Liz for coffee. After two sips into her latte, she was in tears, panicking because her parents were coming from overseas for a visit in a few weeks, and she didn't want them to see the disaster that was her home. To add to her despair, no matter how much she begged and pleaded with her husband, to fix things, he kept telling her, *"Don't worry Bella. It will take me a week tops. It will get done."* This promise was made and deferred weekly, with no movement in the right direction. Liz was getting desperate.

I wanted to get to the root of the problem, so I probed Liz, trying to determine if there was more to the story - maybe their finances were not what his multimillion-dollar home renovation job should reflect? Maybe he had a gambling addiction that left them with crippling debt? Nope – none of those scenarios applied – Manny was simply a procrastinator when it came to getting stuff done around their place. He facilitated everyone else's dream home dreams, except his wife's. Don't get me wrong, he had great intentions, and big plans, but his follow-through was non-existent.

As we chatted about potential solutions to the problem, Liz joked that she should just hire a contractor to get the job done. I thought that sounded like a reasonable idea under the circumstances. And with that, we Googled *"General Contractors, Toronto."* And voila! – we were presented with a long and magical list of efficient tradespeople.

I dialled the first one on the list and handed Liz the phone. Within 2 hours, a contractor was at her home, assessing the requirements of the many unfinished projects, and giving her an all-in-one quote to 'get er' done'. Without consulting Manny, Liz signed off on the quote. It was settled, the contractor and his crew would start the next morning. And you know what? Within a week, the place was a perfect show home!

The craziest thing about this story is that Manny didn't even put up a fight. In fact, he seemed relieved that Liz took matters into her own hands. Liz is clearly, far from useless!

Lory's Two-Timing Timmy

Lory, my long-time dental hygienist, recently discovered that her husband Tim, has a second family. Before sitting in "the chair" at my dentist's office a few weeks back, I exchanged typical pleasantries and small talk with my hygienist of 22 years. Only this time, my usual *"...thanks for asking, and how are you and the family doing?"* reply and follow-up inquiry, were met with a flood of tears. As Lory was cleaning my teeth, she told me the most shocking story I've ever heard.

In Lory's own words:

"Ellie, I'm living the ultimate betrayal of my life, and I'm absolutely heartbroken. My husband Tim, the man who I thought was my rock, my great love, and the best father ever, has been having an affair for over 20 years. Do you know that we just celebrated our 25th wedding anniversary? For Fuck's sake, (excuses her language) *we have 3 kids together - two in college, and our youngest still lives at home. I can't believe that this is actually happening to me — it's like a bad dream. And to make matters a zillion times worse, Tim has a whole other friggin' family, and I just found out that he's been with this woman for almost the entire time we've been together."*

When I took a moment to rinse my mouth, during my cleaning, I asked Lory to start at the beginning and give me as many details as possible.

Lory continued, *"As I think I've told you, Tim is an insurance broker, and his company has multiple branches across the country. He travels all the time with his job, and he usually spends a week or two* (air quotes) *'on the road' every month. Well, it turns out that 'on the road,' is code for spending time with his other family, who happen to live in the same city – about a 15-minute drive from our house! Can you believe this shit?"*

With my mouth open and full of gauze, I still managed, *"What the fuck!"* At this point, Lory's eyes were swollen, and she was getting a little aggressive with the scrapping tool, so I told her I needed a little break. She obviously needed one too. I asked Lory to take a deep breath and finish her story before she finished with my mouth. She moved my chair into the upright position and then she took a seat in a swivelling stool, facing me. With a deep breath, Lory finished her shocking story:

"It was by complete fluke, that I found out about the other family. I have a side business restoring and painting old furniture, so I opened another Facebook profile, strictly for the business, but first I wanted to add some "friends" to give my page legitimacy. Of course, I started by adding my friends, and my husband. When I searched for Tim, a profile I'd never seen before popped up. It was him, but he was using a different last name. And through that weird f'ing profile, I was able to find links to pages of his other family members – a wife and two teenage sons! This insane discovery was only a few short months ago and I'm still in shock."

I asked Lory what she did next, and her answer really took me by surprise. Her actions were calm, cool, and conniving. She handled the whole thing brilliantly; *"I didn't know what to do. It was the most surreal feeling I'd ever had in my entire life, and I didn't really have a plan, but one came to me pretty quickly. At the time of this life-altering discovery, Tim was of course 'on the road,' presumably with his other family. I gave my head a shake and came up with a plan to catch him in the act. I told him that Brenda* (Lory's boss, and my dentist), *gave me a few days off, and a voucher for a 2-day hotel stay with the Marriot hotel chain, because I was* such a hard worker, and deserved a little time away with my wonderful husband.

I told Tim that I had booked the Marriot in Niagara Falls for two days, where he was reportedly on business for the week. Tim validated his guilt by acting all nervous and sketchy. He said, 'Why would you book a hotel room for two days, during the time I'm already staying at a hotel for work? Let's just do it another time.' So, I replied, 'Great point, I'll come today, and stay with you for a few days, and then we can use the voucher another time. And don't worry, I've already made arrangements for Mikey (Lory and Tim's teenage son) to stay with Jane (Tim's sister) for a few days.'

Tim scrambled and said that he had a big work dinner that night, so he'd have to come and meet me at the hotel later in the evening, or perhaps I should just come the next day. I wasn't about to let him off the hook, and I told him that I'd be happy to wait in the hotel room if he'd just confirm which hotel he was staying at, and the room number. I also asked him to make sure to leave a key at the front desk for me. This was all bogus of course, and I knew that Tim would have to scramble to get to Niagara Falls (2 hours southwest of where his other family lived), book a hotel room, leave a key at the front desk for me, then take off for the evening, and pretend to be at a work dinner."

I couldn't believe what I was hearing, but I was riveted to Lory's story and couldn't wait to hear what happened next.

Lory continued, "Tim fell into my trap, and he quickly made hotel arrangements and sent me the details. I acted all excited and told him that I'd have some champagne and another surprise waiting for him when he got back to the hotel room. In the meantime, I was able to do a little digging and discovered that Tim's other woman who was also conveniently named Laurie

57

(different spelling), worked as a salesperson at a car dealership where Tim bought an SUV (for our family) from her about 20 years ago. I guess that's when the affair started up. I called the dealership and confirmed that the other Laurie would be at work that day. Then I decided to pay her a visit.

The other Laurie was as shocked as I was to learn about Tim's double life and two families. At first, she thought my story was part of an elaborate prank that one of her long-time colleagues was pulling. Sadly, when she saw all the digital proof of Tim's and my life together, she was as equally devasted as I was. Long story short, Laurie agreed to go to Tim's hotel room with me. Throughout the day, when Tim would check in with her, she just played it cool, and he was obviously grateful that she was understanding of his last-minute business trip.

When Tim arrived at the hotel room and opened the door, both of us were sitting in chairs, facing the door. I wish I'd recorded his reaction. I swear I could have gained a million followers online if I'd posted that video, which certainly would have gone viral."

I asked her, *"What did he do?"* Lory said, *"He literally turned around and ran. F'ing coward!"*

Just then, my dentist came into the room and asked Lory if she had completed my cleaning. She hadn't, but who cares, her story was more important than my meticulous mouth. I winked at Lory as I said to the dentist, *"Yup she's all done – she did a great job as usual."* Dr. Samuels excused herself and said she was just finishing up with another patient and would be back in a few minutes. This left just enough time for Lory to finish her story.

"This is still so fresh. It's only been 2 months since it all unfolded, and my kids are destroyed by all of this. Tim is gone though. He knew better

than to enter MY house again. He sent his brother Mike to pick up his stuff, and apparently, he's staying at his father's house now. (The other) Laurie said his reaction was the same with her, but she and I have been in touch and talking regularly through all of this bullshit. It's so insane to be living a parallel life with another family, but I'm strangely glad that Laurie and I have each other right now. I think we're the only ones who can truly relate to what has happened. Our kids have even met now because they are half-siblings! How crazy is all of this?"

I had no words other than to tell Lory how sad I was about the whole situation and let her know that I was free to talk anytime she wanted, with or without gauze in my mouth.

Recently I sent Lory a note, just checking in, and I included a link to a Facebook page called *"Are We Dating The Same Person?"* She replied a few days later, telling me that she knew all about it - she said she found Tim on that page, and 3 women (so far) have identified him as their boyfriend. What a useless fool!

Bob 'The Knob'

"How is it possible to have mind-blowing sex with someone you can't stand?" That's how Bette started our conversation, as she recounted the 3 painful years she spent in a totally toxic relationship with Bob.

Bette met Bob at a bar in "the Beaches," a laid-back neighbourhood with a vintage small-town vibe, just 20 minutes east of downtown Toronto. Bette said that although she was wearing the worst outfit of her life that night, she still managed to attract the attention of Bob, a tall, dark, and oh-so-handsome Civil engineer. When he asked for her number, she thought to herself, *"He clearly has no fashion sense, but at least he knows a quality woman when he sees one."*

Bette is a true romantic, and a total sucker for a hot guy who could deliver a cool line, like this one: *"What do you like for breakfast?"* Things moved at lightning speed for Bob and Bette, and soon she was spending most of her free time at Bob's home in the Beaches, which was about 40 minutes east of her place. Bette was a fabulous chef and she enjoyed experimenting with new recipes for her amorous and always-ravenous new boyfriend.

Bette also had a great job in the Arts and Entertainment field, and she introduced Bob to a whole new world of culture, including art shows, live theatre, ballet, and classical music. In exchange for showing him the big, beautiful world of cuisine and culture, Bob introduced Bette to his tiny toddler, Violet, who lived with him every second week since he separated from his wife. Bette was naturally concerned about dating a man with such a young child, but he assured her that his marriage to Violet's mother, Jess, should never have happened. He often compared their bond to the one between Seth Rogen and Katherine Heigl's characters in the movie *Knocked Up.* According to Bob, he and his ex were *"A one-night stand, that produced the gift that keeps on giving."*

Things were great for a while with Bette, Bob and even Violet until Bette realized that their happy and fun life was facilitated entirely by her. When Bob had Violet with him, Bette did everything. She cooked, cleaned, arranged, and paid for all the kid-focused outings, which Bob rarely attended. Bette also became the conduit for pickups and drop-offs with Violet's mom. As time went on, Bob became less and less involved with his daughter when she was "with him."

He started having mysterious appointments on his Violet weekends, and Bette became the primary caregiver. One evening when Bette and Violet returned home from a day at the Zoo, Bette told Violet to go wash up, as she started cooking dinner for the family. Bob returned home shortly after that, from *"running some errands,"* and he scolded Bette, *"Why are you starting dinner at 6:45, Violet should be having dinner at 6 p.m.?"* Bette was naturally pissed off and wanted to leave, but she felt a strong commitment to Violet and didn't want to let her down or leave her in the care of her absent father.

This was a few years into their relationship, and it was as though Bob had Bette just where he wanted her, and now he could do whatever he wanted. Since meeting Bette, Bob had been in and out of jobs, always quitting in a fit of rage, telling Bette (and anyone who would listen), how badly he'd been treated by his employers. And increasingly, Bob became a controlling and abusive a**hole to Bette. He started telling her how to dress, and who she could and couldn't spend time with, and he even started commenting on her weight. She was a size zero, but he was going to make sure she stayed that way, with statements like, *"Are you really going to eat all that?"* and *"Maybe you should change into another skirt, that one looks a lot tighter than it did a few months ago."*

Bob was a master gas lighter, and he was also a serial cheater as Bette discovered one night at a house party. Bette had recently been out of town, in Portugal, for work for nearly 4 weeks, and she was pleasantly surprised to have thoroughly enjoyed her time away from Bob. She felt stronger, well-rested, and less anxious than she had in as long as she could remember. She didn't even miss Bob that much, but she was eager to see and spend some bonding time with Violet, who was now 3 years old.

When Bette arrived at Bob's place, after not seeing him in more than 4 weeks, he didn't bother to welcome her or comment on how tanned and beautiful she looked, and he didn't appear to have missed her much either. He just mentioned that she was late and they *"Should get going ASAP."* As soon as they walked into the house party, which was just 4 doors down from Bob's place, a woman lunged at Bob, yelling at him, *"I can't believe you brought her here. I guess you didn't have the balls to tell her yet, did you?"* Bette was naturally confused and looked to Bob for some answers, but he just shrugged it off and went to the kitchen to get himself a drink. In the meantime, the crazy woman moved on to two other women, and she was engaged in an open argument with both – right in the middle of the room.

One of the women caught Bette's attention and waved her over. There, the three women heatedly told Bette that she was just one of many women in Bob's life and that they had each been sleeping with him for some time.

At that point, Bette knew what she had to do. She quietly walked away and out the front door of the house party. She walked to Bob's house and gathered up her personal effects. Not wanting to leave any trace of herself behind, she decided to inadvertently *'take back'* anything she had given Bob over the years. That was almost everything. Armed with a set of kitchen shears, Bette methodically went from room to room, cutting up sofa cushions, throw blankets, area rugs, and clothing (including many of his silk ties), and she managed to break every adult-sized plate in the house. She thoughtfully left all the (piles of) stuff that she bought Violet over the years, untouched.

When Bob returned home about an hour later, he was in shock at the carnage within his home, at the hands of gentle Bette, and he realized that she had finally had enough of his bullshit. He begged her for forgiveness and tried to convince her that his bad behaviour had nothing to do with her, he just felt insecure because of his *"bad luck"* on the job front and was looking for some unhealthy attention. Bette took his pleading in stride, and she even led him to believe she would forgive him. She told the loser go upstairs and, *"I'll meet you there in a few minutes."*

When she got upstairs, Bob was in bed naked, and touching himself. I guess conflict and toxic relationships really turned him on. Bette grabbed a few of his uncut silk ties and ordered Bob to spread his legs and his arms wide open on the bed. As Bette slowly slipped off her black lace cocktail dress, revealing the very sexy bra and tiny panties she was wearing, Bob told her how hot she looked, and that he couldn't wait to be touched by her.

Bette played along. One by one, she tied each arm, then leg to a bedpost, then she blindfolded him. Bob professed that at that moment, he was more sexually aroused than he'd ever been in the 3 years they'd been together. While he was begging for Bette to touch him, she sat down beside him, and whispered in his ear *"I'm sorry Bob, there are just too many people in this bed."* With that, she got off the bed, put her sexy dress back on, gathered her things, and walked away from the now wriggling Bob, and out of his life forever. Before she left the bedroom, Bette glanced back quickly, to see that the knobs on Bob's bedposts had all fallen off, in his struggle to try to free himself. She chuckled to herself as she thought, *"Bob the knob. How fitting."*

A few weeks after this scene, Bob's ex-wife called Bette and told her how grateful she was for all that she'd done for Violet in the years that she'd been in the little girl's life, and that she wished for her to stay in touch with Violet. Bob's parents even called her, mourning the loss of Bette's presence in their family. His mom Jane told Bette that she always knew that she was too good for Bob, and better off without him, but if she wanted to come visit them at their lakefront cottage sometime, she was more than welcome to bring a new man with her.

Bette told me that looking back on their relationship, she'd known almost from the start that she and Bob were doomed. But like most good and decent women, she ignored the signs, until it was too late.

6

SEPARATION – LET THE (HEAD) GAMES BEGIN

"I approach most endeavours with zero expectations, which is a skill I have honed after forty years of regular disappointment."
– Samantha Irby

After I separated from my husband(s), my first exhaustive lesson in being a single mom revolved around "pick-ups and drop-offs." We, moms, pick up our kids (from hockey, karate, ballet, tennis, gymnastics, swimming lessons, kid yoga, piano lessons, dreaded play dates, multiple weekend birthday parties, tennis, etc.), we pick up the teacher and coach gifts, we pick up the many holiday duties (including playing Santa), and we pick up all the extra slack. Men somehow drop off the Earth when there's heavy lifting to be done.

I must admit my "guys" were pretty good at the pick-up, and drop-off thing when our kids were younger. Sharing 50/50 custody with my two baby daddies was pleasantly smooth in this one regard. They took their pick-ups and drop-offs seriously, and for that, I was always grateful. With little to contribute to this endless female topic of discussion and frustration, I turn it over to the ladies who have suffered real pick-up and drop-off frustration.

Emily's Story (in her own words)

"It's no coincidence that the pick-ups and drop-offs of my kids seem to depend on the weather. If there is a snowstorm, I can guarantee that my ex will have to work late. Conversely, when the weather is really nice - and by really nice, I mean really nice drinking-on-a-patio weather - a client meeting

somehow surfaces at the last minute. I can hear his excuse in my head: 'I really have to meet with some important clients tonight, so can you please do me a solid and pick up the boys? This is really important!' Of course, I can pick up the boys. Every time. Because it's either me or Child Protective Services. Duh!

And don't even get me started on the number of late notices the boys have had on their school attendance records. On the mornings that Michael drops the boys to school, I will hear the buzzing on my iPhone around 9:05 a.m., like clockwork. It's the school. It's always the school, wondering if they can expect the boys today or if they'll be late or absent yet again. When I ask the school why they don't contact Michael about this, they tell me that Mike has informed them that 'all kid-related inquiries are handled by their mom.' Is he useless, or what?

And then there are the extracurricular activities. Honestly, you'd think Michael was the one who had to play soccer or perform in the Christmas pageant. His whining and pure disdain for attending anything his children participate in, is unnerving: 'Do I really need to go?' or 'Max won't miss me,' or 'It's just a bunch of 7-year-olds, and I've got so much to do already.' And, on and on it goes. He does everything in his power to get out of taking the kids to their 'stuff.' He doesn't see it as part of the job, and it always becomes my problem to pick up his slack.

I just keep telling myself that someday all this hard work will pay off. One day, I know my boys will see that their mom is awesome and that their dad's a bit of a deadbeat – though I'd never say this within their earshot. My great hope is that by leading by example for them, they will grow up to be able, loving, polite, and generous men...with big paychecks, yachts, mansions, with fountains overflowing with gold - and they will take good,

good care of their mama and spoil her rotten. I also hope that they will never ever get married and… well, a mom can dream at least, can't she?"

Single Dads vs. Single Moms

The phrase "It's my weekend off" has a very different meaning for single moms versus single dads. Dads literally have from Friday morning (after the school drop-off), until Monday evening (before the school pick-up), kid-free. During that time, they can do whatever they like. They can even leave the country if they want. The kids aren't their problem. Moms, on the other hand, are rarely afforded that luxury. Moms are perpetually "on-call," and always ready to jump in to lend a proper parenting hand.

In this regard, like with pick-ups and drop-offs, my single dad vs. single mom situation has been mostly a pleasant exception. When my relationships ended, I quickly learned how to put my foot down when it came to my time off. *"Sorry fella, it's your weekend with the kids – I'm sure you're more than capable of dealing with it"* became my mantra.

Making the men take responsibility for their offspring has made them better dads, because they've had no choice but to manage the responsibilities that come with children - including managing their ongoing drama, roller coaster of emotions, their extreme messiness, their picky appetites, and infinite requests; *"Are we there yet"* and *"Can I have X?"* In short – I've become just fine with tuning out and letting them tune in to their children for 2 whole days, every second weekend.

Jan's Man

My friend, Janis, may as well still be married, although she's been legally separated for nearly a year now. And while she and her so-called ex, Praveen, live in separate homes, and have a legal and binding document clearly stating that she gets every Thursday evening and every second weekend free from her kid duties (and all to herself), their separation arrangement, is anything but separate. He's always at her door dropping the kids back home, mid "visit" with Dad.

As mentioned, Praveen and Jan have been "consciously uncoupled" for nearly a year, yet Jan has not been able to enjoy two days in a row, to herself. Something always comes up that prevents Praveen from being able to take their daughters for more than one night, even on weekends. There's usually *"an emergency"* at his work (for the record, he's a banker, not a heart surgeon), or Praveen has forgotten about a very important commitment to just about anyone and everyone else, that not so conveniently prevents him from spending any real time with his kids. It's endless. And Jan is always mentally and physically exhausted.

There is a silver lining to this story, though. Being the "NO!" pro that I had to become to find some of my own freedom, I had a little chat with Jan about putting her foot down. I told her that she needs to stand up to the guy and tell him that when it's her time off, he may as well assume she's out of the country, and if he needs a babysitter - to hire one! It took Jan another few months to work up the courage to stand up for her right to have a life. She needed a monumental event to shake up her perceived obligation to accept that

68

she'd have no kid-free time in her life, to facilitate her useless ex's livin' la vida loca 24-7 life.

When Jan and I were out one night with a few other women for drinks, a handsome younger man approached Jan, and they chatted for about an hour. When we left the bar, she was on cloud nine, thrilled that the young hottie had asked her for her number. It was the next day when he called to ask Jan to dinner, that she suddenly had no trouble telling Praveen to shove his emergency dinner meeting, *"where the sun don't shine,"* because she had a *"date with a hot younger guy"* that night.

Praveen was so blown away by her boldness, and newfound self-confidence, that he never asked Jan to take the kids during her time off again.

Out Of The Marriage, But Not Out Of The House

When I first separated from Hubby Number 2, he refused to leave my house - the house that I owned, the house where I was raising my 3 kids, with no help from him, the neighbourhood where each attended a different school, and the area where all their friends lived. This is the house where Number 2 merely paid a small portion of "rent" as he liked to call it, towards my massive mortgage. In fact, this joker even drafted a "Rental Agreement" before he moved in, stating that he'd commit to paying a small amount of money each month, and in the (likely) event that our relationship did not last, he would have no interest in my interests, if you get my drift.

When things predictably went south in our relationship, he decided to squat, even though it meant that the rest of the family (me and the 3 children) would be out on the street. Charming, huh? Due to our increasingly volatile relationship (the man-child liked to punch holes in walls, and kick down doors), and the fact that he refused to vacate my home, I was forced to pack up the 3 kids and move out. I rented a small 3-bedroom townhouse across town, for a few months, until I could have Derek legally, and forcibly removed.

During that time, Mr. "More Of Everything" took full advantage of the wines I'd cellared, the cable and specialty channels I paid for, and the Olympic-sized pool in the backyard. He loved to host barbeques and entertain his many deadbeat and useless guy friends, and he threw several high-class cheap beer and Polish barbeque sausage parties.

Also, during that stretch, I managed to drop off and pick up the children at their respective schools, take them to all their events, and keep our lives, as drama-free as possible. The only way I was able to have my ex-dud forcibly removed from my house, was to sell it. I bought a much smaller home in the neighbourhood – all in a concerted effort to keep my demanding chauffeuring duties to a minimum, and my sanity in check. Number 2 still managed to get half of the proceeds of the house, but I was finally able to wash that man out of my life, and my graying hair.

Lyla's Losers

"I wonder if men and women really suit each other. Maybe they should live next door and visit now and then" - Katharine Hepburn

I met Lyla at work many (many) years ago, and we became instant besties. Today, even though we each have kids, jobs in different professions and crazy lives, we still manage to get together at least every few months. Recently, we were reminiscing about the good (and bad) old days, working for a big advertising agency in Toronto, as account representatives (aka "Suits").

In those carefree, but unhealthy (and now illegal) long workdays, Lyla and I spent a lot of time developing product pitches, launching new products, attending promotional events, and entertaining clients. Regardless of the day or night, there was always a party in full swing, and no expense was ever spared. Our big clients (fashion brands, pharmaceutical companies, luxury car companies, etc.) had deep pockets, and our monthly retainers were ridiculously high. This meant that our duty to keep our clients happy, translated to a lot of late (sometimes sketchy) nights, involving a bottomless supply of booze, and a bevy of party boy clients with expensive suits, and cheap pick-up lines.

At some of these parties, Lyla met men who were eager to impress her with fancy dinner dates, expensive gifts, and promises of longevity. Needless to say, Lyla test drove several relationships. Some were good – but mostly short-lived, and others were downright disappointing. For some reason, the disappointing ones seemed to be the ones with staying power.

"I was always flypaper for freaks" Lyla recalled at our last night in. This sad truth is perplexing, given that some 20 years later, she's still a stunning woman with a great job, a wicked fashion sense, and a killer sense of humour. In my eyes, Lyla was every quality guy's dream. Yet, for some strange reason, she attracted (and was attracted to) men that only mothers could love – and even then, I'm sure the mothers were only too happy to pass their sons her way, and out of theirs.

71

Over an open bottle, I opened a can of worms when I asked, *"Hey, whatever happened to Steven?"* For years, Lyla went out with one jerk who had a fantastic (high-paying) job, a beautiful big condo, overlooking Lake Ontario, and no dependents. That's where the good stuff ended. For some bizarre reason, even after many months into their apparently "exclusive" relationship, Steven never let Lyla spend the night, and he rarely picked up her share of the tab for dinner – even when he insisted that they dine at super fancy restaurants.

When Steven was at Lyla's place, a pretty and cozy one-bedroom, he took full advantage of her generosity. He hounded her to buy a treadmill because he hated the gym (he didn't want to pay for a membership, and the one in his condo building was always packed). He also encouraged her to buy all the streaming apps – because "his favourite shows" were spread across all of them.

I know I'm hardly one to talk, having put up with similar behaviour from the man-child, but at some point, you'd think she'd have just said, *"Enough! I'm not married to you, you're stingy, you have commitment issues, and I'm too good for you."* Finally, after 4 long years, she built up the courage to sell the space-taking treadmill, take back her remote, and finally move on from soul-sucking Steven. The breakup was anti-climactic. And, apparently, Steven is married to a man now.

And Then There's Todd

One day, Lyla met Todd. He was adorable! He had giant dimples, funky blond hair, great personal style, and a cool job in the film business. What more could a girl want? Indeed, Lyla fell head over heels, and they enjoyed 6 romantic, and incident-free months of proper dating. Then Lyla got pregnant, she married the man with the dimples, and they lived happily ever after... Well, not quite.

About a month after her wedding (and while she was five months pregnant), Lyla discovered that Todd was up to his eyeballs in debt. He'd maxed out every credit card he owned to the tune of about $100,000. His condo was owned by his parents (to whom he owed six months of back rent), and his production company (which he "owned") was taking a huge hit during the recession. Lyla's dream man turned out to be a bigger nightmare than the last bozo.

When she had the baby, Lyla had to return to work six months early from her maternity leave as a fashion magazine account executive, just so that she could cover her family's mounting bills. And it seemed like the more she worked, the less Todd did to contribute. He'd lie around on the couch all day watching movies, and his excuse was always, *"I'm just waiting for a call from a client . . . a big account is coming in babe, big account."*

Todd's wardrobe and director's lifestyle didn't suffer, though, during these tough times. He always managed to go out for drinks a few nights a week, and he often walked in with a new sports jacket or a cool new pair of "kicks." Todd always justified that he needed to *"look the part"* to *"get the parts."* Lyla worked herself to the bone, trying to provide for herself, her new son, and her lazy, self-absorbed, useless husband.

After nearly three years of toiling and heading into near bankruptcy herself, Lyla decided to cut her losses, take her toddler, and move out. To make the separation as painless as possible for their son Ben, Lyla rented a two-bedroom condominium in the building next to Todd's new bachelor studio (read between the lines - no room for baby Ben at Todd's Inn).

Things between Lyla and Todd were going well, all things considered. They found that the time and space apart was good for them and their son. They had a renewed friendship and enjoyed each other's company far more than they had before, as Lyla no longer had any unmet expectations. As the months went on and the friendship grew (neither were dating yet), Todd realized that the comforts of home were only really felt at Lyla's.

This story would be sweet if it turned out that Todd's undying affection for his wife couldn't keep him away from her for long, but sadly, it was her big screen TV, stocked fridge, and liquor cabinet, that helped Todd realize that there was no place like (her) home. Todd also liked the fact that Lyla's place was Ben's primary residence. Ben and all of his toys lived there most of the time too, which meant that Todd's tiny condo was a solo, clutter-free haven. Todd also made a point of leaving Lyla's, for his own home, just before Ben had to be bathed and put to bed.

As time went on, Todd started spending more and more time with his son at Lyla's place. And soon, he just started coming "home" to Lyla's after work. He'd help himself to her food, her booze, and her TV. He became so comfortable that he felt no guilt about kicking Ben off the couch, so that he could spread out and watch movie after classic movie, on all of Lyla's streaming networks.

It wasn't until Lyla started taking advantage of her contractual "every second weekend-off" arrangement that things started to change. She met someone. He was a real gentleman, named Dev. He was a bit older and financially secure, and his kids were grown and out of the house. Dev insisted on picking up the tab for dinners, and he never let her open her car door. He even took Lyla on romantic weekend getaways. Lyla's newfound freedom helped her to establish some boundaries with Todd, which included him caring for Ben at his place.

One night, after a dinner date with Dev, while Ben was supposed to be staying at Todd's for the weekend, Lyla decided to take her new man of several months, home to her condo for the first time. She thought it would be a good idea for Dev to see where she and her son lived, before actually taking the next big step, by introducing him to Ben.

So much for that. When they walked into her freshly cleaned place, the vision of Todd lying across her sofa - engrossed in a movie, eating leftover pizza in his boxers, wearing her Ugh slippers, while drinking her wine - was enough to send anyone over the edge. But it was her discovery of Ben playing alone in her bedroom with a big bucket of finger paints, that stole the show. That, and the fact that he was also feeding spoonful's of CheezWiz to his action figures, on her new bedding.

The time and space continuum had finally come to an end. *"No more time together, and lots of space between us"* became Lyla's new mantra when it came to her ex-husband. A few months after this episode, Lyla was pleased to report that once she put her foot down, Todd stepped up, and out of her space for good.

7

SAD SACKS

"Man serves the interest of no creature except himself"
– George Orwell

When you've been in a relationship for a while, you learn to accept that sex doesn't always have to be earth-shattering. A quickie can be hot and fun, and it can give you BOTH a small taste of what's to come, when you can find time for a proper romp in the sack. The problem is, when your man only seems to want quickies, or he is all about "me" and not "me too," he's the only one who exits the roll in the hay, feeling satisfied. When I put this delicate subject out to the universe of partnered women, I had an overwhelming number of blunt responses, from dissatisfied ladies.

I Can't Get No...

When I asked Trish to share how the sex was with someone that you've been married to for over 20 years, she didn't mince words:

"I've lost the will to tell my husband that he totally sucks in bed. His ego and self-esteem are so delicate, that commenting on anything that he: cooks, makes, wears, or even observes, is taken with complete sulking self-absorption, unless it's over-the-top positive - and we've been married for 20 years!

I'll start by telling you that I'm very lucky, in that it doesn't take much ' work' for me to have an orgasm. However, I feel like my husband takes advantage of this and does the bare minimum when it comes to my pleasure. Sex is very one-sided, with me always being the only one performing oral sex, stimulating him manually, and even giving him erotic massages. I try, I mean I really try to please him, and trust me, he is ALWAYS satisfied. But, when it comes to my needs, if I don't orgasm during intercourse, I'm out of luck. During our last encounter, he orgasmed during oral stimulation, without reciprocating. He just turned over and went to sleep, while I was left to 'finish myself off' with my vibrator. Here's the best part - the selfish jerk actually had the nerve to ask me to 'take it into the bathroom' because the buzzing was disturbing his sleep.

In the past, when I've tried to discuss sex with him, it has led to impotence and no real progress. My husband has been in therapy for a while now, and when I've asked him how it's going, he says 'It's not, just leave it alone, if you please.' I think that a more fitting response from him should be, 'Pleasing you? I think I'll just leave that alone.'

He's All That...

Guila once went out with a guy who had mirrors – lots and lots of mirrors, in his bedroom. Thankfully, they weren't fastened to the ceiling, not that she'd have noticed, given her boyfriend's preference for doing it doggy style, while looking at himself in the mirrors.

Guila is a funny, funny girl. Like me, she loves to relate everyday situations to scenes from popular movies. When Guila was telling me about her 4-month tryst with the man in the mirrors, aka "Narcissus," she couldn't stop laughing. She said she hated watching herself get pounded from behind, but it was hard not to catch a glimpse of herself with all the mirrors around his bedroom. However, the expressions that Narcissus made while he was enjoying himself,

77

always reminded her of Christian Bale's character, "Patrick Bateman," in the movie, *American Psycho*. Guila said that he would contort his face, flex his muscles, and point at himself in any one of his many mirrors, mid-coitus. She also told me that while she hated the sex, she found him supremely entertaining. *"Narcissus really thought that he was all that, and a bag of chips - though the show would have been more enjoyable with some popcorn."*

Cecilia's Sex Education

When I heard this sad story from an acquaintance who was only too eager to share her tragic tale of sexual unhealing, these famous lyrics by The Beatles, kept playing on repeat in my head, like a broken record; *"Oh Cecilia, you're breaking my heart..."*

Cecilia started, *"I have been with my husband for roughly 7 years and married for 4. Our sex life is just terrible, and it has slowly descended into a dead bedroom over the last 3 or so years. The thought of living like this for the rest of my life is so utterly depressing and isolating. I'm not sure what to do.*

When we first got together, I had considerably more sexual experience than Ed, and I took a lot of control in the bedroom. I put in SO much effort — to be sexy, to make him feel sexy and to allow him to explore new things. I put a lot of time into getting to know his body and giving him intense pleasure. Sadly, Ed's always been a passive recipient, and it took me a long time to realize that he has never made any effort when it came to pleasing me.

I have tried to guide him and teach him about what I like and don't like, and what works for me. It has been a long, frustrating, and even painful experience. He doesn't bother to get me wet; he can't find my clitoris, he literally jams his fingers into me at weird angles, he does the typical jackhammer move (his only move), and he has no concept of rhythm. Trying to teach him how to have sex, has failed time and time again, because he just can't seem to retain the knowledge or the skills. I have never faked an orgasm with him, and I've tried to openly communicate how our sex life could be so much better if he'd just slow down and pay attention to my responses. As the years have gone by, and none of my teaching or communication has helped, I have grown to really dislike sex.

In the past few years, I have had 2 conversations with him about needing more from him in the bedroom. He took the first one well and said that he was embarrassed, and for a short time, he made more effort to satisfy me. The second and more recent conversation (a few months ago), has resulted in him just giving up. He doesn't initiate sex at all, and now when I try, he just walks away, locks himself in the bathroom, and masturbates.

As a result of all this, I have started to feel a lot of resentment towards Ed, and I'm at my wit's end. I just know that I will end up divorcing him eventually if this situation doesn't get fixed. I wish desperately that there was some kind of sex school that I could send him to, where he'd learn the ropes (or at least the basics) on someone else's body, with a skilled teacher. I would gladly pay for this type of service, and I would not feel an ounce of jealousy — only relief, and a small glimmer of hope that he'd get a passing grade, and some transferrable skills."

The 6 Million Dollar, 2 Second Man

"Jane," my neighbour, is married to a rich guy. She's about 25 years younger than her husband, and there's no doubt that she married Richard, ("Rich") for his dough. One thing I've noticed about Jane is that in social situations, especially when she starts drinking, her gums start flapping. I ran into Jane one night at a local pub. She was with two younger, equally attractive female friends, and I was with my teenage daughter and her two friends.

The kids were there for the wings. I was there for the local entertainment. I popped by Jane's table to say a quick hello. The ladies were enjoying some cocktails that were freshly purchased by some hunky young men at the next table. I asked Jane if the guys knew that she was married. She admitted that she didn't care and said, *"Rich gave me the night off. He got his 3 pumps of pleasure in this morning, and he's good for the next month, so I'm free to flirt my ass off* (chuckling), *until the next uneventful occasion."*

8

THE SONS OF US BITCHES!

"God did it on purpose so that we may love you men instead of laughing at you." – Mrs. Patrick Campbell, in reply to a male acquaintance who asked why women seem to have no sense of humour.

Again, the title is harsh, but when you have a useless son or two, and you're bold enough to call them out on their bullshit, Mama gets labelled a "B." Like my friend Emily says, *"When you have no expectations, you can never be disappointed."* The trouble is, when a mom goes from having no expectations, to suddenly expecting her sons to know how to cook, clean, sew, and do their own laundry, we really have no one but ourselves to blame for the useless men we've raised.

My son "Hank" (his nickname, and what I've called him since birth) is a bit useless, but as I said, I only have myself to blame. I have babied the heck out of the guy. He's almost 17 and I still offer to cut his meat into little pieces. And, when no one is around, he lets me do it! Don't get me wrong, he's a sweet, sweet guy, but he couldn't make himself a sandwich to save his life. He would starve. He's already so skinny, and just thinking about it makes me want to start boiling water for his favourite pasta.

Oh, my darling boy... your Mama has done you so wrong! If only you'd been born during the cavemen days, or in the wild, wild west, none of this useless man stuff would apply to you at all. You'd be able to skillfully hunt, kill, and provide for your little Freddy Flintstone family, or you'd be able to sling a gun and fry up some mean muskrat if it came to that. I could carry on about my useless son, but I just can't. I love him too much. He's my baby boy, he is so "Hanksome" and whoops, I'm doing it again.

At this point, I'm sure there's a witch hunt out for me, and I can certainly understand why, although I'd hope that everyone who's reading this book, regardless of gender, understands that the big message I'm trying to share is that despite men's shortcomings, I, and the rest of the feminine collective, still love and adore men (for the most part), and we certainly can't live without them. The proof? We keep having them, dating them, marrying them... and doting on them! As Hank would say, *"That's a total fail, Bruh."*

As you can tell, I really adore my son. He is the man of the house, and he's a great pal of mine. Hank "gets me" better than my two girls do, and by a long shot. We can spend hours together watching TikTok videos of stupid pranks and stunts, and our favourite mom-son bonding time, is watching ridiculous B horror flicks, and all the Jackass and Furious (5,6,7...) movies – all night long. We can also make terrible and almost cruel fun of each other, all in the name of one-upmanship, and our mutual ability to laugh at ourselves.

Just last week Hank was telling me that I'd better be prepared for some backlash from the mere title of this book. I told him, *"No problem, babe. I intend to use a fake name."* He said, *"What name?"* (and under his breath, *"This should be good"*). I told him that I could just use my bar name – the one I used to give to guys (along with my fake phone number) when I was in my 20s. *"Ellie Russo didn't write this book, Paige Wrigley did,"* I proudly declared. Without missing a beat, he said, *"You mean a page that's old and wrinkly, don't you?"* I nearly peed my track pants, laughing. And with that, I realized that although I still think the opposite sex is useless, women still need them for great comic relief and a sense of perspective.

Another funny thing about a mother-son relationship is the incredible candour that boys have when it comes to "private" stuff. Teenage girls are truly horrible in this regard. If you want to know anything about their lives, you have to "creep" their social media accounts (if you can find them), and if you're really lucky, you can find, and read their journals… NOT THAT I'D EVER DO THIS ☺.

While driving my lazy son the mere two minutes down the road to school one morning, I asked him if there were any girls he liked, besides Léa Hélène Seydoux-Fornier de Clausonne (aka Madeleine Swann, the Bond girl – ahem, woman) – whose posters he has plastered all over his room. He said, *"No, not really, but my friend Aaron is having sex with a 19-year-old."*

Naturally, I was a bit shocked by the casual revelation, but decided to play it cool; *"Oh yeah? How do you know he's telling the truth?"* He said, *"Oh because Brandon and Nathan watched the video that she uploaded to Porn Hub… I can share the link if you want to see it."*

I was speechless but also grateful, knowing that when my little boy becomes a man, I'll likely be one of the first to know.

Wife, Mom – It's All the Same in Sickness!

This story is a real oldie but still a goodie…It's a fact - a mom is expected to feed her kids, take them to school, pack their lunches, make dinner, bathe them, buy the groceries, and do the laundry… all while suffering a 102-degree fever. A dad gets the sniffles, and he may as well be dying.

Okay, ladies, here's the truth – men are babies when they're sick. Women, on the other hand, aren't allowed to get sick. However, I'm "sick as a dog" (my kids hate that expression) right now, because I've been infected by two all-night projectile pukers in my home, for the last 48 hours. Though I've had to make a few pit stops to the can myself, before delivering my children's trays of dry toast and chicken broth, my only saving grace is that I'm too stuffed up to smell the barf that permeates their bedrooms, and the entire house.

There was a great commercial a few years ago, for Nyquil Cold and Flu Relief medication. It went like this: A man is lying in bed, feeling under the weather, and he's practically sobbing. His wife is in the washroom, looking at him with slight disgust. When the hubby says something to the effect of *"Pam, call my mom – I think I'm dying,"* Pam responds by throwing the useless dud a bottle of Nyquil. Every woman, married or connected to a man in some capacity, can relate to this commercial. It's brilliant. And because we all know that women are the only ones who actually think to purchase medication in advance of minor family illness, the commercial is spot-on to Nyquil's female target market. The agency that produced this spot deserves an award – as does the (most certainly) female writer who wrote the script. Bravo!

As I said, I'm pretty sick right now – where do you think I get my inspiration for these topics? My son Hank, and my youngest girl "Bagoo," also have the flu. Of note, Bagoo is my baby's real nickname, but she goes by "Goo" for short though, because in my crazy household, even the nicknames have nicknames. As my family's martyred matriarch, I like to refer to myself as "Cindy," short for "Cinderella," of course.

Lately, Goo has been sleeping with me, in my bed, every night. This isn't really that out of the norm anyway. She goes through phases where she's in my bed for weeks at a time. Her beautifully decorated pink bedroom and white sleigh bed have remained untouched lately, and we all affectionately refer to Goo's bedroom as "the museum." It's a hazard of being a single mom, I guess. You can get the man out of your bed, but never the kids. Honestly (and selfishly), I wouldn't have it any other way – she's the best little cuddler in the world. She's also an amazing patient to care for when she's sick. Even as she's reaching for "the bucket" at the side of the bed, she doesn't make a peep. My sick son Hank, on the other hand, is a big baby.

Hank loves to watch Netflix when he's home sick from school, and because I have the only bedroom in the house with a TV, he's moved on into my bed, and taken over the clicker. All I can say is that because Goo is ill, she's been going to sleep with relative ease, so the *Black Mirror* marathon that's been lighting up my bedroom at all hours of the night, is quietly playing without too much fuss from me or her.

Last night (the second night of both kids sleeping in my smallish, queen-sized bed), Hank started to cough. It wasn't just any cough – it was the *"I'm about to barf"* cough that every mom can recognize instantly. Stretching myself over Goo to reach for and hold up the bucket to catch his projectile, the little man decided to turn his head and shower me and his sister with the most horrifying explosion of puke I've ever experienced. I screamed at him, *"In the bucket Hank, in the bucket!"* But Hank just kept puking on us – dare I say, almost at us! One good whiff and I knew I was doomed.

85

Sprawled over both kids, all of us (well less so Hank) drenched in his puke, I hit the bucket with my own violent explosion. Of course, it was only a matter of time before Goo was next. Rubbing her eyes and sitting up in her barf-soaked princess dress (no nighties for this kid), she said, *"Mommy, my tummy hurts."* With that, she jumped out of bed, and bolted for the washroom. Stripping off my own puke-soaked clothes and heading into the washroom after her, I was amazed to see this incredible little girl, leaning over the toilet, ensuring that not one drop of (her substantial) vomit hit anything but the bottom of the bowl. When she was done, she wiped her mouth with toilet paper, threw it in the toilet, and flushed. Not one sob, moan or look of agony.

Equally efficiently, she proceeded to take off her soiled Cinderella dress (the irony of this once again would have me nearly peeing my track pants if I was still wearing them), and she asked me if she could have a bath. I said, *"Of course, baby,"* as I turned on the water. While the bath water was running, Goo reached into the cupboard under the sink and pulled out two little bottles, then she threw in some bath salts, and bubble bath, as I headed back to my bedroom to assess the damage and see if Hank was okay.

"I don't think I can move, Mommy," Hank said (for the record, I hadn't been "Mommy" for years), as he shielded his eyes when I turned on the light. Getting a good look at the devastation to my 400 thread count sheets, and everything else within Hank's shooting distance, I nearly projectiled again. I said *"Come on Hank, it's disgusting in here and so are you. We need to get you out of here and cleaned up."* He replied, *"I'm not having a shower in the same room as that brat."* Clearly, he was not dying. I told him I'd get a shower running for him in the other bathroom, but that he needed to get up right away so that

I could clean the sheets, walls, floor, furniture, and everything else he managed to hit – all so that we could get back to sleep and start to feel well.

With a single tear running down his face, Hank whispered, *"I think you need to carry me, Mommy. I'm too weak."* Just then, Goo peeked around the corner of my bedroom entrance, with Hank's puke now crusting in her hair, and with a sweet little smile, she said, *"I turned off the water, Mama. Are you coming to sit with me while I have a bath now?"* What more can I say here?

Spoiled / Rotten

Have you ever known (or heard of) a kid who was "spoiled rotten?" I recently learned that there is a medical term for this. It's called, 'The Spoiled Child Syndrome.' This is a condition where a child displays excessive self-centred and immature behaviour due to the parent's failure to enforce consistent and age-appropriate limits. However, there are outlying reasons for the behaviours that concern parents, that are not related to spoiling. These behaviours may just be normal for the child's age and stage of development (see Chapter 11, "The Teenage Daughter Years"), reactions to family stress, or due to inherent factors of a child's behaviour. Unfortunately, the stories to follow are not entirely the result of parents who refused to set boundaries with their children or follow through with consequences of their bad behaviour.

Mad Max

My son's former friend Max, and his family, are very wealthy. They live in a huge house, have a lakefront cottage, they frequently purchase new luxury cars, and they take multiple first-class vacations abroad every year. Max is one lucky kid, and his parents never deny him anything. Max is also not surprisingly, "spoiled rotten."

When iPhones were first becoming popular, this spoiled rich kid desperately wanted, no "needed," one. He asked his parents for a phone in a specific colour, but it was close to Christmas and that colour was sold out everywhere. His mother was disappointed that she couldn't find the exact phone Max wanted, but she managed to convince a customer at the mall to sell her his new phone, as it was very close in colour to the one her son wanted. She paid the man double the price he had paid, and she was certain that the gift would make Max happy.

Fast forward to Christmas Day. Max eagerly opened the box containing his brand-new iPhone. However, to his disappointment, Max discovered that the phone was not the exact colour he had hoped for. Frustrated with the situation, Max impulsively threw the phone to the ground, causing the screen to crack. He also lashed out at his mom, calling her a *"Lazy bitch,"* for not getting him exactly what he demanded. After this outburst, Max stormed off to his bedroom without opening any of his other (zillion) presents.

When Andrew (Hank) told me about this incident, I asked him how he knew all the dirty details. He shared that when he went to Max's house late on Christmas Day to wish his family a happy holiday, their live-in housekeeper, Luisa, was in the process of moving her belongings out of the house, and into her car. She was crying at the time, and Andrew offered to help her carry her things to the car. Luisa then divulged the unsettling details about what had transpired that day. Luisa had been working (and living) with the family since Max was a baby, and she felt that she had earned the right to speak up when she witnessed Max's temper tantrums and other truly terrible behaviour. She had had enough of his deplorable antics, and she wasn't going to turn a blind eye to them, especially on Christmas.

After Max smashed his new phone, Luisa followed him to his room and scolded him for behaving like a completely, *"spoiled, ungrateful and abusive son to a mother who does everything for you."* Max was in shock and for the first time, speechless. He had never been scolded by his parents, let alone mild-mannered Luisa. Luisa mentioned to Andrew that she could tell that Max's mother, Christine, was relieved to finally have someone stand up for her and reprimand her son. However, Max's father, Ben, had a different reaction. He quickly intervened and put Luisa in her place, reminding her that she was not a family member and that, *"No one speaks to my son like that - no one!"* He also told Luisa that she was *"...free to leave if you have a problem with it."* Luisa had a problem with it, so she left.

From that moment, Andrew could see that the spoiled rotten apple didn't fall far from his father's tree, and he decided then and there, to end his friendship with Max. Andrew told me recently that he ran into Max's mom at the movies. She appeared to be on a date with a nice–looking and attentive man. When she saw Andrew, she gave him a big hug and a quick update. Apparently taking a page out of Luisa's book, Christine decided to speak up for herself, letting both

89

males in her family know that she was done with being treated like garbage, and they were welcome to have each other to rely on from now on.

Before the new year, Christine had moved out and moved on. That was several years ago. Apparently, Max (who is now 23), didn't bother to finish high school, and he's still the same spoiled rotten brat, just older, fatter, and balder now. He's jobless, still living at home, and mooching off his now miserable and useless father.

A Truly Bad Seed

Warning: *This story contains content that some readers may find disturbing.*

When my eldest daughter was enrolled in a treatment program for adolescents struggling with addictive behaviours and other mental health issues, I quickly realized that as a parent of a troubled teen, I was not alone. Many kids were far more troubled than my Jules. Mental health issues, addictions, and sometimes just plain old DNA are the imperfect elements for the perfect storm of self-destruction. All families involved with the program, spent a lot of time in the eye of the storm, before finding clear skies.

Although that stormy time was several years ago now, the circumstances surrounding one particular boy in the program, have continued to haunt me. As a result, I decided to reach out to the family to see how they are doing now. Sadly, there is no happy ending to their story. The mom of this troubled boy passed away from cancer a few years ago, and his father made a conscious choice to give up on his son.

I asked the dad if he would mind sharing their story, and he agreed. This is not the story of a useless father, although some could argue that no matter the circumstances, a parent never (ever) gives up on their child. However, in this truly tragic father-son relationship, I think it's more a case of "survival of the fittest."

Shawn and Kelly's son was very problematic, to put it mildly. If you've seen the movie, *"We Need to Talk About Kevin,"* it will help you understand the magnitude of issues that Kevin (no small coincidence) suffered, and inflicted, on everyone around him. When Kevin's dad, Shawn saw the movie he said, *"I swear to God when I watched that film, I thought I was watching a documentary of my family's life. I felt like the writer must have had cameras hidden in my damn house - that's how accurate the story was to our real life."*

Shawn continued, *"From the day he was born, he was wanted and loved. We showered affection on him, and we really tried to give him a happy childhood. But from the moment we brought him home from the hospital, he was miserable. Kevin cried for 13 months straight. There were times that he would literally be crying in his sleep - I've never seen or heard of any other kid who did that. We brought him to doctors, and specialists. We tried changing his diet, we held him, rocked him, gave him toys, swaddled him, played music. We did basically anything and everything we could think of to make this child comfortable and happy. Nothing worked.*

As soon as he could walk, Kevin's mission in life was to destroy things. He would break anything that was within his reach, and this continued through adolescence. Between ages 9-14, he bullied other kids at school, and he was repeatedly suspended, and then finally, expelled. He got

91

into drugs and alcohol, and he became extremely violent with everyone who crossed his path (myself and my wife included). By the time he was 14, Kevin's behaviour had become dark and criminal. He was caught several times destroying public property and breaking and entering homes and businesses. The police became a daily fixture in our home. We had no idea what else he was up to, but we knew it wasn't anything good."

Shawn told me that it took more than a year on the lengthy waiting list for Kevin to be accepted to the same treatment program as my daughter. When Kevin was admitted, Shawn and Kelly were thrilled that he would finally be getting the help he needed, from some of the best mental health professionals in the country. While Kevin was away from home, life became peaceful for his parents. Unexpectedly, Kelly got pregnant. However, instead of being joyful about this news, *"We felt pure terror,"* Shawn confided. He continued, *"This pregnancy had not been planned, and we were terrified that this child would be like Kevin."*

At the same time, while Kevin was in the program, he repeatedly ran away, was caught, and returned. He managed to get his hands on narcotics and shared them with some of the other boys in treatment, and he was denied any type of contact with the girls in the program because he repeatedly threatened them with rape and other violent acts. Everyone, including the professional staff at the treatment facility, were afraid of Kevin. According to Shawn, *"To be honest, although my wife went to visit Kevin every third Sunday for a few hours on the premises, I just gave up and cut all contact with him. I think I was trying to preserve my strength and mental health for the birth of our next child, and I know that I was suffering from PTSD."*

Kevin was still in treatment when his baby sister was born. Shawn said that with his second child, *"Everything was different this time. She was a happy, healthy, 'normal' baby. I can't describe the relief and happiness that my wife and I felt, I don't have the words for it. We cried tears of joy for the first time in 15 years."*

The remainder of Shawn's story is very grizzly, and hard to fathom:

"For the next few months, Kelly and I focused on our baby daughter, while Kevin was focusing on how to escape treatment. It clearly wasn't working, but at least he was in the right place, should he finally decide to participate in getting better. When our daughter was about 2 months old, I went to visit Kevin for the first time in many months. I tried to connect with him on some emotional level and I shared happy stories about his baby sister. I lied when I said that we loved him. I told the truth when I said that we needed him to get well, so that he could come home, and we could all be a family.

With dead eyes, he looked at me and said, 'I don't have a sister, or at least I won't for long.' With chills running down my spine, I left my son, went home, and told my wife that we needed to move, immediately. I was prepared to literally run away from Kevin and never look back. I didn't want him near me, my wife, or our daughter. I was being a bad parent for the first time, but I didn't care anymore. I knew that he could kill us.

We agreed to move in with my brother (who lived in another province) for a while, until we could figure out where we'd settle, and where we could place Kevin until he was an adult. We just needed to feel safe. That night, as we were packing up some clothes in our bedroom, we heard a piercing cry from our baby's room. We ran to her and saw Kevin standing over her crib, with a steak knife in his hand. I don't know how he got in, or where he got the knife from. I think he may have stolen it from one of our neighbour's houses. As the baby wailed, we could see that she was bleeding from her foot, belly, and face. He looked up at us and smiled.

Before I was conscious of what I was doing, I was already moving, running to put myself between Kevin and the baby. I got to our son and smacked the knife out of his hands, and I shoved him against the wall and held him there. The look on my son's face was blank and cold. His eyes were dead. As I pinned him against the wall, I yelled at my wife to take the baby, who was still screaming, and to call 911. Before the police could arrive, Kevin managed to break free, and out the door.

Thank God our daughter's injuries were superficial and did not require stitches. From that moment, I knew we needed to get away from Kevin for good. We moved out that night, and we never bothered to search for Kevin or even report him missing.

All of this happened several years ago, and I carry some guilt and conflicted emotions about running away from our son, but I believe in my heart that we did what was right for us, and for our daughter."

9

BROTHERS NEED MANY MOTHERS

"Of all your great achievements - that fake cry that made our parents come running, is what makes me most proud of you"
... Said every older sister to their 'baby' brother

Useless men come in many packages. They're not just dads, boyfriends, hubbies, or sons. Brothers can suck equally too. The proverbial "they" say that when a young man starts dating, he subconsciously seeks out a girl who has the same qualities as his mother. According to a recent study by dating site, eHarmony, 64 percent of men seek a serious relationship with someone who shares significant personality traits with their mother. And from an evolutionary, and psychological standpoint, this makes perfect sense. Relationship expert, Rachael Lloyd, shares that *"With moms as our primary caregivers in life, it's no surprise men are attracted to women who possess similar values."*

During my brothers' formative years, our mom increasingly relinquished her motherly duties to me, and to a lesser extent, my older sister. We were the ones who did the heavy lifting when it came to making sure our brothers were bathed, dressed, fed, and played with. As we (and our single mother) got older, and eventually left her "nest," our mom took that opportunity to move out of town and live a child-free life of her own.

While my brothers were technically adults at the time, they were still in search of motherly caregivers. And those caregivers manifested themselves in loving and doting girlfriends, and later, wives. That is, until the wives got sick of the one-way-giving experiment they tested out (called "marriage"), and eventually became ex-wives. So, what then?

In my case, and for many other sisters with brothers like mine, my brothers (especially Jay, the elder of the two), sought too much of my attention to fill their neediness. Sisters, after all, in their minds, were the next best alternative to an absent mother.

Dinner With Jay

Since his divorce, getting a dinner invite to my brother Jay's house is rare, and it usually entails me bringing the groceries, cooking a fine meal, and supplying some good vino. However, the alternative to me preparing the feast, is to suffer through his famously undercooked frozen pizza, and boxed wine. Having three kids to drag along with me to these rare events, has made catering to Jay in my own home, more practical, and literally much easier to stomach. What's one more kid anyway? And unlike the clear perspective, and intolerance I now have for these types of lazy men, blood is blood, and my useless brother(s) get the occasional pass.

On a positive note (for my brother), when Jay is visiting, he feels very much at home. He has confidently secured his own, specific place at the table, he's commandeered the comfiest TV-watching chair, and he even "stores" a small beer fridge at my house (I don't drink beer), that he's somehow manipulated me to keep fully stocked for him.

It's funny (not really), but when my brother Jay got married, he made sure to select a take-charge kind of woman. She's a lot like me. She efficiently managed their household - the finances, the food, their daughter, and their schedules. She had their lives running like a well-tuned machine. It was not without its drawbacks though. The more Tracey did for Jay, the less and less he contributed. At some point, Tracey decided she'd had enough of his bottomless pit of incompetence, and she left him.

Conversely, my other brother Ry, married a woman who was the spitting image of our mother in her heyday. They, too, are separated now. Amazingly, I have a great relationship with my brothers and, separately, my sisters-in-law. And I actually prefer them better, apart.

"Baby" Brothers

In my personal experience, the curse of feeling perpetually guilty is usually reserved for mothers. There's never enough of us to go around, especially if we work full-time and have kids. For this reason, many of us moms bend over backwards, split ourselves in half, and try to be everything to everyone – all at once.

But sometimes, after an extended absence from one's wife and kids, a man can start to feel guilty too. A while ago, when they were still married, my youngest brother's wife and her 2 boys, came to spend the weekend. My brother Ry, had to work all weekend, and Jenn wanted an escape from her usual, trapped-at-home-with-two-wild-boys misery.

Needless to say, our moms and kids' weekend was a blast. We let the younger kids run wild, despite that the house looked like a bomb had gone off, just thirty minutes into the 48-hour visit. As usual, on this of many weekends like it, Jenn and I paced ourselves, limiting our wine intake, to not render us completely incapable of making the countless meals and snacks for the little vultures, but also, we drank just enough to keep us amply numb to the constant whining for "*More of everything, Mommy!*" My youngest daughter had been taught well by her manipulative older brother, how to get just about anything she could ever want from her exhausted Mama. How could I mind, though? Soon enough, she'd have her own spouse and children to split herself in half for, and she'd be the one who was giving more of everything.

By the end of our long 2 days together, Goo begged me to let the boys stay over for "*Just one more night!*" She rationalized that it was a long weekend anyway, and there was no school, or work to wake up for the next morning. As usual – she won. Besides, the extra day off meant that I could take the whole following day to clean up and try to restore the house to its pre-long weekend glory.

Once the decision was made to make the most of our "Just one more night" together, the call came in. I guess Daddy was finally starting to miss his little family, and he thought it was time for them to "*Come home.*" He had to go to work again in the morning and wanted to spend a few hours with his wife and kids, before having to hit the road at daybreak. It was obvious that Ry's weekend fun was over (there were always copious after-work drinks with the production crew who he worked with), and it was an opportunity for him to ease his guilty conscience and "play house" on a Sunday night.

When Jenn let him in on our extended weekend plans, Ry made a strong case for himself, telling her that he'd had to shoot outside all weekend, and he felt like he was coming down with a cold. What he really wanted, was for Jenn to come home (now) to baby him and wipe his runny nose. She almost gave in too, but when she saw the look of sincere disappointment in the eyes of her wild boys and my Goo, she found her inner strength and told Ry to go hit up the pharmacy, for a bottle of Nyquil Cold and Flu Relief.

Life Is Tougher "Up Here"

While I take some delight in delivering pot-shots at both of my "little" brothers' expense, they are two of my closest friends. Jay is the soft one, who constantly works to build my self-confidence with sweet little lies, and compliments about how pretty I (still) am. Ry, on the other hand, is the only dude I know, who will give me the painful truth, like, *"You need to lose ten pounds,"* or *"Maybe you should rethink those leather pants, Ellie."*

Ry is also the source of many of my fondest memories as a kid. Having had an unusually rough week at work (both he and I), we had a sweet and mutually supportive text exchange. Recalling one of our fondest childhood memories at our small island cottage, I texted, *"Don't you miss the days when you were catching bullfrogs in the swamp all day, and I was acting out the story of Rumpelstiltskin at the foot of your bunk beds, at bedtime?"* His response was funny, spot on, and touching all at once; *"Yes - it's much tougher up here now."* I took his reply to mean that life was carefree and easy as a young boy, versus the crushing responsibility-filled world he must endure as a grown-up man, with a mortgage to pay, a job to keep, kids to care for, and a wife to please. Never mind the stress of having to keep up with the Joneses, if you're someone like my brother Ry. It really is *"tougher up here"* for someone like him.

Sometimes, we efficient moms, wives, and career women give these big boys no slack. I think we expect so much from them because we accept nothing less than perfection from ourselves. I will always have a soft spot for my little brothers and their challenges as grown (ass) men. Their inability to consistently deliver the goods as dads, partners, and brothers, is not surprising, considering that they used to spend long summer days catching bullfrogs in a swamp and cooking bugs through a magnifying glass, only to be interrupted by the call for lunch by their loving mom, and responsible sisters.

10

HORRIBLE BOSSES

"Sometimes it takes balls to be a woman" – Elizabeth Cook

The Bad, The Good, And the F'ugly

Throughout my long and colourful marketing and communications career, mostly working for Fortune 500 companies, I've had some pretty shitty male bosses – like I mean, really shitty! They weren't so much useless as they were; arrogant, dismissive, unempathetic, misogynistic, entitled, cruel, narcissistic, controlling, sexist, inappropriate, unrealistic, demanding, and a whole slew of other atrocious descriptions, that don't come close to encapsulating my full experience, working for (many) men.

By contrast, the man that I work for now, as a Content Designer for a Canadian bank, is hands down, the best boss I, or anyone (male or female), could ever hope for. He is smart, talented, creative, professional, empathetic, caring, fun, and a true leader. He has restored my faith that great male bosses do exist in the real world, and his exceptional treatment of me (and everyone else), has given me the courage to revisit some (post) traumatic (stress disorder-causing) working environments of my past.

doG, ssoB - It's All The Same In A Dyslexic And Dysfunctional Workplace

Here's the truth, I am dyslexic. Often, I tell my jokes out of order, and sometimes, they even work...

Q: *Did you ever hear the one about the super son of a bitch (ssoB)*
       "Boss" who was a horrible, and offensive "doG" to his female staff,
       but was revered as a "God" amongst his male colleagues?

A: *Who hasn't?*

My First But Not My Last

The sad truth is, that most women have had at least one horrible boss. Unfortunately, I've had more than a few. My first job was my introduction to the world of bad male bosses, and he was by far the least horrible of the bunch.

When I graduated from university at the ripe old age of 21 and landed my first real job in the marketing department with a theatre company on the West Coast, I thought I had it made. The marketing group was a fun, colourful, and eclectic bunch. The big boss was a nice, refined middle-aged gentleman, whom I called "Mr. Johnson" (out of respect, of course). He was very handsome, with just a touch of grey at the temples, and he had a very soft charm about him. I loved working for the theatre, and for Mr. Johnson, although there were a lot of late nights and plenty of hard work, for poverty-line wages. I was okay with that though. I was getting amazing career and life experience, and the perks included unlimited tickets to top-notch theatre productions, and mingling with some of Canada's finest actors, directors, and social elites.

About 5 months into the job, I was thrilled to suddenly be getting the attention of the theatre's Managing Director, Mr. Johnson, much to the dismay of the other junior marketers in my department. In no time, I went from "Girl Friday" to "It Girl." And my job title unjustifiably changed from Associate Marketing Manager to Director of Audience Development. *"Damn, I must be good,"* I thought. One late (late) night, Mr. Johnson called me to his office to talk about the success of the latest packed performance of *"Little Shop of Horrors."* Having had a few celebratory glasses of champagne, and feeling proud of my recent contributions, I took the bait.

While he didn't make any moves on me that night, he did ask me if I'd mind accompanying him (professionally, of course) to some upcoming galas. These were high-profile events, with mass media coverage. I was flattered and certain that he was developing feelings for me. Otherwise, why would Mr. Johnson be okay with being photographed with little old me? Having recently finalized a divorce from his long-time partner, Sharon, being seen and photographed with another woman, was a serious commitment after all.

As the months went on, we attended several events together, and our pics were splashed across the Arts section of every major newspaper. Mac (as I started to call him) was always a perfect gentleman, although he did start getting overly comfortable with me, asking me for favours like dropping his tux to the cleaners, picking up his shitzu, "Mitzy" from the dog groomers, grabbing lunch for him from the market next door to the theatre, etc., etc.

I naturally thought that Mac was old-fashioned, and he was just taking things slowly, to see if we could have a real connection. I was also honoured that we had formed the type of close relationship where he felt that he could depend on me to do whatever he needed – professionally, and personally. With this understanding, I lapped up my assigned chores with enthusiasm, appreciating that I had the attention of the West Coast God of the live theatre world. I happily helped him with whatever he needed me to do, knowing that one day, it could pay off for my career.

Day after day, the personal tasks kept flowing in, and my real job started to feel less like an Audience Development Director, and more like something out of the Nanny Diaries. I needed to know if this 'thing' that we had, was heading into real relationship territory because my task-running usefulness was killing me. One evening after another packed show, I put on my tightest black skirt, highest stilettos, and a way-too-low white blouse, and I marched into Mac's office to get my answers, even if it meant that I had to sleep with the old and powerful Oz. Imagine my surprise when I found Mac, with his "Johnson" out, locked in a mad, passionate kiss with Tommy, the theatre's bar manager. *"Wow! Checkmate,"* I thought. I'd been played - and well.

It turns out, that Mr. Johnson (and his "Johnson," that I'll never be able to unsee) was using me as a beard for photo ops all over town. He was very much in the closet and wanted to keep it that way publicly. The best way for him to do that was to string me along and make me feel like girlfriend material. By having me do girlfriend-type stuff, and deal with his dirty laundry, so to speak, he was fooling the world, and me, at the same time.

The revelation was too much reality for me. So, with my tail and my ego tucked between my legs, and my first taste of the real world behind me, I packed my bags, hopped a plane home to Toronto, and left the theatre world for good.

The Ageists

When the COVID-19 pandemic hit, I was "temporarily" laid off from my job of 5 years, as a Senior Marketing Manager and Content Lead, with a private (old-school) energy company. The bosses/owners were misogynistic old fuddy duddies, who had no problem expecting the women in the marketing department to pick up their lunches, make their dinner reservations, buy their wives Christmas gifts, and even help their teenage sons with their school assignments.

Professional respect from these old boys, was something reserved for the men in the office, and the owners treated the mostly female marketing department, as a mad-man-esque secretary pool of domestic resources. On a professional level, we were all just part of an expendable cost centre, that didn't contribute much to the bottom line.

I was the first to go. As the oldest woman in the department, I had the most experience, and I made the most money. Before that dreaded phone call from HR, the company had me working 16-hour days from home, for the first month and a half of the pandemic, converting their rusty (and a tad bit shady) door-to-door sales structure, to a digital platform. They had no choice. The pandemic was pushing these outdated duds into the digital age, and I was the only one in the company who had the experience to get them up and running, fast.

As soon as the switch "flipped on," and their websites (4 in total) were open for online business, I was very casually canned, and informed, "*It's just temporary.*" It was not just temporary, and they immediately cut me off in every way. They denied me physical access to pick up my personal items (including my one and only winter coat, and pair of boots), they refused to return any of my calls or emails the entire time I was on "temporary layoff", they immediately cut off my health benefits, and they did not pay me one cent of severance.

These jerks were using the term "Temporary Layoff" to skirt their legal severance requirements, and they were just waiting me out – hoping I would find a job somewhere else, and they'd be relieved of their financial obligation to me. Not surprisingly, a few other mature women in the company were also let go, regardless of experience or tenure. Also not surprisingly, every useless (and I mean USELESS) man's job remained intact.

Bills to Pay, People to Sue

As a single mom with 2 kids in university and another teenager at home, the bills were becoming staggering by month 5 of my unemployment, despite my frantically searching for a new job, in an abysmal market.

I was so angry, and I was getting desperate to bring in some cash! Although I didn't have the money, I still managed to lawyer up and sue the heartless crooks for constructive dismissal. I won, but the severance package barely covered the debt I'd racked up while unemployed.

I managed to secure a new job after 7 months, however, at the time, the job pickings were very slim. There was a surplus of newly displaced and experienced marketing "talent" fighting for the same few jobs. Worst of all, and not surprisingly, the wages appeared to be about half of what they would have been prior to the pandemic. It seems that COVID became the opportunity for companies to slash salaries and dump loyal, older employees, regardless of their experience.

The job I landed was as a marketing and communications writer with a tech company. My salary was less than what I had made in more than 20 years, yet I felt lucky to have found a job. Sadly, most of my similarly displaced female friends were still looking, more than a year later.

New Job, New Hope, New Set of Micromanaging Headaches

When I started my new job with the tech company in late 2020 (a few weeks before Christmas), I had no clue what I'd be in for. I joined a lean team of 6 people, with a painfully micromanaging young male boss. My workload was that of 3 to 4 people, but I managed to keep up. Remember, I was used to working 16-hour days, evenings, and weekends, and I'd always prided myself on getting the job done.

By month 3 of this monstrous, never-ending workload, under a manager who was low on praise but big on giving direction and constant "constructive" criticism, I realized that everyone in my department had abandoned me. After doing a little digging, I discovered that I was the 5th writer in my exact role, within a 2-year period. This "Baby Boss" as I referred to him (only in my head, and under my breath, of course), couldn't keep staff. The turnover was constant, and I had to keep "helping" new employees find their footing. I felt like the Baby Boss was trying to push me out too. He was incapable of giving positive feedback, and he kept lumping project, after project, on my plate.

Of course, I worked harder and harder (and harder), in an attempt to keep up, and to hopefully win him over. It never happened. Even when I had my performance review and received a perfect score in each measurable category, and my blog posts increased traffic to our company website by 130% (the goal was 15%), that still wasn't good enough. So...I finally gave up, and found another job, and pretty easily actually. And... Halleluiah!, I really liked it. As the old saying goes, *"It's always easier to find a new job when you already have one."*

(Real) Letters to My Editors

When you're a writer (which I am, and I do for a living), the pen is truly mightier than the sword. As I've gotten older, and less tolerant of deplorable behaviour, I have used my words to get the last word, so to speak. I've found that freedom of expression has been therapeutic and almost vindicating when targeted in the right way.

Over the years (including very recently), I have written some mighty powerful exit letters to those who thought it was okay to unjustifiably and inappropriately "edit" me. That is, to edit; my work and my ability to work, my appearance, my personality, and especially my comfort as a woman, and human being.

Mostly, I've received no replies to my letters, but I do know that they were received and read (read receipts are so satisfying, aren't they?) – and that's good enough for me. Here are a few of my favourite letters (emails) to my editors:

Re: The Micromanager

Good afternoon ███,

I did not have the pleasure of speaking with you, although I did attend the ███ Town Hall in January, where you were speaking, and I was impressed with your plans for the company in the upcoming year.

I am writing you now, to share my story as a former employee of ███ (as of yesterday). It is important that you absorb what I have to say, as what has happened to me is completely unacceptable... and I will NOT go quietly into the night. I hope this will have some impact on you as the leader of a large organization. I'll share bullets to assist you with the background, my timeline with the company, and the series of events that brought me to compose this letter.

- When COVID-19 hit in 2020, I lost my job (5 years as a senior marketer with an energy company, before that I was a Director of Marketing with another energy company). As a single mom of 3 kids, I need to work. The market at that time was saturated with senior/experienced marketing talent who also found themselves in a similar position – laid off, and with very few jobs to apply for. The salaries, not so coincidentally, were much lower than in recent years too. I put out a ton of resumes, interviewed with ███, and was offered a job as a Senior Content Specialist. The job title was very junior, given my experience, and the salary was about half of what I had previously made, however, the job description was very robust, and its duties could only be properly fulfilled by someone with extensive experience (like mine). The bottom line is, I needed a job, and I took it. I started on December 12, 2020.

- The head of marketing at the time was an inspiring guy. He pushed to get me more money than the role was offering, as he knew I deserved it, and he assured me that with my talent and extensive experience, I'd go far in the company. He also told me that with a bonus, I'd be making decent money. With a massive salary cut and a huge leap of faith, I joined ▮▮▮▮▮ as the organization's solo marketing and communications writer and strategist. From the time I accepted the role, to the time I started, the role's title was downgraded from Senior Content Specialist to just Content Specialist. It was annoying, and a tad humiliating, but again, I needed a job and was locked in by that point.

- When I started, I worked on the company's 3 distinct lines of business – ▮▮▮▮, ▮▮▮▮ and ▮▮▮. I wrote all customer-facing content (blogs, whitepapers, emails, traditional and direct marketing campaigns, I helped sales executives with their 100+ page RFPs, I created content strategies and full marketing plans for each line of business, I wrote ▮▮▮▮'s vision statement, I wrote scripts and I art directed videos, I interviewed clients and wrote case studies, brochures, sell sheets, internal communications, social media, webinars, etc., etc., etc.). The volume of work I was given, was that of at least 3 people in my professional opinion as someone with over 25 years of experience. Somehow, I managed, and I flourished in this overwhelming role. I more than rose to the occasion but I was also running on fumes… working 16-hour days and every weekend - whatever it took to complete my tasks – and complete them WELL (feel free to read any of my blogs and other content on the ███████ site to see the excellent quality of my work!) The company eventually split into 3 separate divisions, each with its own content role. I stayed with ███████, as it was the largest division. My workload continued to be massive, but I was well into the swing of the role and was pumping out content like a well-oiled machine.

- Within my first few months with the company, nearly everyone quit marketing. ███████, the head of the group - moved on, the Salesforce Manager, ███████ took sick leave, the graphic designer, ███████ left the company, the events person, ███████ moved to another team, and most recently the web guy, ███ – left the company too. At less than a year with the company, I was the longest-remaining employee, other than ███████ – the Senior Manager/boss of the department. ███ is a smart man, and he is clearly passionate about his work. He is also a mentally and emotionally crippling micromanager who is ill-equipped to distinguish the amount of direction needed by him to a new (fresh out of university) employee, and the amount of direction needed for someone with decades of experience, who's run large marketing departments before. His exhaustive micromanaging style has been painful to endure. I was professional but vocal when his deplorable treatment became too much, and I often opted to let things slide because I knew deep down, ███ doesn't mean to be so toxic – he was just incredibly controlling. Everyone

111

who's worked for ▮▮▮ would say the same thing – he's smart, he's hard working, he is extremely over-managing, and he never ever takes ownership of his mistakes. He's a gaslighting expert. It gets exhausting. THIS however is not my issue. I had a few discussions with HR throughout the year about ▮▮▮'s behaviour, when I found my circumstances intolerable, and my attempts at expressing my concerns directly with him did not work. These issues went unaddressed. I gave up, I kept my head down and continued to "produce" like the machine that I am. For the record... I think ▮▮▮ has the potential to be a people leader, with some extensive soft skills/sensitivity/EQ training. That's my professional advice. Take it or leave it.

- As 2021 was ending, I was almost desperate for a salary review, and a well-earned bonus. I had given everything to the company that I could. My blogs were driving traffic between 98-132% each quarter – although my goal was to increase traffic by only 15%. The first webinar I created and organized on my own for ▮▮▮▮▮▮▮▮▮ was also a massive success. These are just two small examples of my work success and work ethic. On January 25th I received a year-end performance review. I got a perfect (all 10s) score in each category that I was measured on. In my time with the company, I had never taken a sick day, I had far exceeded my goals, and I had impeccable relationships with all my colleagues, as well as the clients that I worked with on a regular basis. I could not have done better, nor worked harder. I felt proud (and well-deserving). ▮▮▮'s comments about my performance were nice on paper although, on our weekly status call, he did offer that it's incredibly rare that an employee gets an all 10s on their scorecard, so perhaps I wasn't challenged enough. I cried after that meeting when I should have been celebrating. Deflated is the only word to describe how I felt.

- At the end of my performance review, I asked ███ about my salary review. He said that wouldn't happen, nor would there be talk of a bonus until mid to late February. My employment contract clearly stated that I would get a salary review and a bonus in January. I'd already been with the company for more than 13 months – at the same pathetic salary of ███ It is unacceptable. I have felt used to say the least. And with the glowing review I received (under a boss who is near impossible to please), I was also quite surprised that there was no discussion of a promotion or anything positive for me – just a giant pile of *"new challenging work "* to look forward to in 2022. This was not what was discussed with ███ when I started.

- On the upside of things for me, I recently interviewed with a few other companies (who pursued me - the market is VERY hot for employees now). I decided to accept a role that pays what I'm worth. I was deep down hoping that magically, there'd be a promotion and big pay jump after my performance review, and I could stay. NOPE. That didn't happen, so I had no choice but to accept another job offer and give my notice.

- Last Thursday, (in my one-to-one weekly meeting with ███), I told him that I would be resigning. I gave my 2 weeks (plus a day) notice. Immediately after that meeting, per

113

▮▮▮▮'s instruction, I sent my notice to ▮▮▮ and cc'd ▮▮▮▮ ▮▮▮▮▮▮ (HR). When I resigned, my boss's response was *"Well your decision is probably for the best."* Again, I felt totally deflated, gas-lit, and unappreciated.

- With just two weeks left to go, and a pile of new work (including organizing another webinar), I decided to give it my all, even though I'd be walking away without a salary increase or bonus, that I had rightfully earned. ▮▮▮ didn't tell me what the raise or bonus would be, but he did manage to let me know that I would have been disappointed – apparently, it wasn't going to be much. By this point, I was feeling down-right abused.

- Two days ago, I submitted an expense for $300 (for my Wellness Benefit) but was told by ▮▮▮▮▮▮▮ (HR) that because I had given notice, I was no longer entitled to reimbursement for my expense. I told him that that was ridiculous. He sent me a one-liner from a document buried within ▮▮▮ that qualified his rejection of my expense. I, in return (quite upset by this point), told him that the company did not honour their own contract with me, by giving me my promised salary review, and bonus in January. I had a labour lawyer confirm this, and I said as much. Then it was "crickets" from his end.

- The next morning, (yesterday) – I received a slack message from my boss asking if he could speak to me for a minute. I said 'sure' (as always), and when I answered the call, he and the HR manager, ▮▮▮ were on the call. My boss did not speak on that call. The HR manager told me that effective

114

immediately, I was no longer an employee with ███████████. From there – there were a few other exchanges with him:

- An email confirming that I'd been terminated (not sure of the exact wording) and that I'd still get paid for two weeks, and some instructions about taxes and pay stubs. He cc'd the IT manager in that very sensitive, humiliating email. That is TOTALLY unacceptable. I told him this. Again, "crickets".

- I asked about my health benefits and when they'd end (my youngest child has regular physiotherapy – I need those benefits for the next two weeks). He said they were terminated immediately (he later corrected himself per the rules of the Employment Standards Act – which I sent to him).

█████, I have been an A+++ employee. To say that I am a professional, kind, and over-the-top helpful person, is a complete understatement. Ask ANYONE at █████████ who has worked with me, or any one of our clients, what their opinion of me is, on all levels. I have no doubt that their review would be exceptional. I thought the company had potential. I think many of the people are smart. **I think the treatment I've received (from the start, and especially most recently) is deplorable.** This is NOT the treatment others have received when they left – and especially the men who have left. No - they were given farewell lunches and gifts. This is wrong. And I rightfully feel discriminated against. You need to know this. But what's done is done.

In speaking with my lawyer, he shared that I have a very strong case for constructive dismissal, if I choose to pursue it. I have decided against going that route. It's better for my mental health to just walk away, and it is most certainly a win-win for you and ▓▓▓▓▓ for me to "just drop it."

I'm on to greener pastures, a bigger and MUCH better-paying job, hopefully less burnout, and certainly a whole lot more respect. As I was not permitted to give an exit interview, consider this as such.

I wish you, and most of my now former colleagues, well. It would have been nice to say farewell. I do hope that you read this, take it to heart, and address my issues. I am not a martyr. I will not let this go unaddressed for the sake of others who may find themselves the subject of this poor treatment in future. I am telling you all of this because you are a leader, and this stuff needs to be remedied from the top down. As you know and as Steve Jobs lived by, *"People don't leave bad jobs. They leave bad bosses."*

Thank you for your time.

Ellie Russo

Re: The Bully

Dear ▓▓▓▓▓,

Unhealthy working conditions at ▓▓▓▓▓ over the past several months have convinced me that I must resign from my position as Director of Marketing with ▓▓▓▓▓, effective immediately. When I was initially hired, I thought that this was a company that believed, as I did, that a relationship between an organization and its employees, should be mutually beneficial. This has not proven to be the case for me.

I can say with complete conviction that I have done my very best to establish a strong and lasting brand, I have built Canadian and

American websites and all communications channels (internally and externally) to promote and propel ██████████'s distinction in a confusing and competitive marketplace, and I have reached long and hard to grab the low-hanging fruit (leads/opportunities) with minimal budget. I know that **I have given it my all.**

I believe you have a tremendous team with potential that is infinite. The young talent you have acquired is second to none, and you should be very proud of this and them. What I do not believe in, is a culture where bullying and mixed messages are, in any way acceptable or tolerated. ██████████'s behaviour is completely toxic, and abusive. I have enough life, and professional experience to say this with complete confidence and conviction. I am a professional marketer. I have managed large teams within massive organizations, with huge budgets, and I am proud to call my former employees - my dear friends and professional allies.

My leadership style has always been 'divided and conquer' - empowering people to deliver greatness - is what I am all about. ██████ sadly, leads by fear, not example - and for some reason, he is particularly verbally abusive to the women within this organization.

I, and every other person who works at ██████, should not have to endure bullying, when we come to work. Crying in the workplace is also not normal. It is not okay. It is inexcusable. I have witnessed far too much crying, perpetrated by this man, who is a total bully. Enough!

I think you are a lovely person ██████. You are incredibly smart and driven, and I admire your passionate entrepreneurship. It's inspiring. I think ██████ is also a great leader, who treats his colleagues and his employees with respect and kindness. Dealings with you both, has been enjoyable and productive. This is the type of leadership that makes people love where they work.

Under ███████'s "leadership" I (honestly) can't thrive. I literally shake when I walk into the office and see him – and I'm not easily rattled. No one should have to tolerate an environment where every idea, suggestion and effort is perpetually challenged, then dismissed. Constructive criticism is healthy and welcomed, but unjustifiable tongue lashings are appalling. This is not an environment I am accustomed to, and I am incredibly undeserving. I am VERY good at what I do, I know who I am, and I know my incredible strengths, and my guidable weaknesses. I am never afraid to ask for help because that serves to foster collaboration and greatness - there just needs to be faith to hand over the reins sometimes!

I was also very disappointed to have accepted a position where I thought I could (and to date, know that I have done) great things. During my review, I was expecting a bonus per my contract. I was counting on it in fact - having left a position that paid me market scale - to enter a segment that was new, vibrant, forward-thinking, and viable - a great challenge of a lifetime - where I knew I could succeed if only given the endorsement of those who hired me, to deliver on my promise - and ultimately reap the rewards. That bonus was never honoured, so I asked ███████ for a copy of my review (understanding that many others received a bonus) and was dumbfounded that this never materialized, based on the very positive feedback I received from you. I can only assume that ███████, as my direct manager, did not sign off on a bonus for me.

There is no point in elaborating - it's an exercise in frustration and futility at this stage, and my decision to leave has been made. Again,

I would like to reiterate that working for YOU has been a pleasure, and I wish things could be very different. You have a gold mine of talent within your organization, that I hope you can respect and nurture to their fullest potential.

All the best,

Ellie

To: The Narcissists

██████,

It is with great enthusiasm that I tender my resignation from ██████ ██████, as Senior Marketing and Communications Strategist, effective immediately. I've taken a much better job with one of your competitors, so per the terms of my contract, today will be my last day.

It's wonderful that my skills are transferable. My dignity, however, is not. As soon as I can pack up my thermal travel mug, Tupperware, cactus plant and my self-respect, I'll be out the door. I've left the company's laptop and my entry pass on my desk, for you to pass along to your next victim.

I wish you and the rest of the narcissistic, misogynistic, and unprofessional male leadership team, nothing but – well, "nothing" is enough, I guess.

Adios,

Ellie Russo

P.S. I'll be sure to write truly crappy reviews on LinkedIn, Glassdoor and Indeed about my experience working for █████████████, and don't worry - I won't forget to backlink to your website, in my next blog post, about horrific work environments, and shitty male bosses.

Maggie's Megalomaniac

"The only people who get upset about you setting boundaries are the ones who benefit from you having none." - Author Unknown

"We all thought he was a famous designer, but it turns out, he was really just a kids' shoe salesman." This is what my friend Maggie told me, as she recounted her days working for an extremely well-known and "talented" florist to the stars. Maggie is a super-talented floral designer herself. Her work is magical, original, and completely tailored to the personalities of her clients. She's also finally in a place in her own career where it doesn't hurt so much to remember the worst boss she's ever had.

For four long years, Maggie toiled in the soil for Davon. His celebrity clients included the likes Cyndi Lauper, Bill Clinton, Cher, and Sting. At least once per week, these types of celebs would send their minions into Davon's shop and ask for something fabulous and, of course, completely original. These projects took time, incredible talent, and they were very pricey. Time and time again, Maggie and her co-worker Mary, would churn out truly one-of-a-kind arrangements. These masterpieces would often be delivered backstage after a concert, or to a hotel suite, and each cost between $2,000 to $5,000+.

Every time one of these arrangements left the shop, a thank you card would arrive the next day for Davon, praising him for his incredible talent, and usually begging him to become <insert super star's name>'s exclusive florist. This was all well and fine for Davon, except the pace by which Maggie and her equally talented co-worker Mary had to churn out these masterpiece arrangements, was nothing short of feverish, and it was starting to feel a lot like free labour.

After three years on the job, and still earning little more than minimum wage - all for the opportunity to apprentice with one of the biggest floral guns in town, Maggie knew that she had to ask for a raise. She decided to try the "worship him" approach, to get what she needed. Davon was always too busy and certainly too cranky to carry on a conversation with his florists unless, of course, it was in praise of his greatness. So, Maggie decided to lead with a question about how Davon got his start in the business, and then hopefully move into the compensation discussion.

Maggie began, *"Davon, you have such an incredible following,"* Then, *"I hope to get to your level someday. Where did you get your start?"* Glaring at Maggie as though she had a third eye, Davon snapped at her and said, *"If you feel you need to question my credentials, then maybe you're not Blooms' material, after all."* With that, Maggie slinked back to her work station and finished her work for the day, her tears adding some sodium and minerals, to her gorgeous arrangements.

After that (non) incident, Davon moved Maggie to the back room, leaving her to create her magic out of sight, and hopefully out of his clients' minds. Through those months of solitude (Mary remained silent, and therefore she was able to remain front and centre in the shop), Maggie began to realize that she'd never actually seen Davon construct one single arrangement, though he had no problem taking full credit for everything that left his shop.

After months of soaking floral oasis, stripping roses of their dangerous thorns, and even cleaning the shop's toilet, Maggie became very depressed and doubtful that she'd ever get her day in the sun. Her anger and desire for justice were also mounting by the day. However, it wasn't until a competing superstar florist, "S," came into the shop one day, that Maggie got her ultimate revenge.

After hearing a heated argument between the two rivals, S's parting words rang in her ears like an angel's lullaby, *"You'll never amount to anything more than the kids' shoe salesman you were when I found you, Darren! I don't know what you're paying those poor girls, but it can't be enough to put up with your prima donna bullshit. Oh, and good news - I hear Zappos has an opening – you're gonna' need a job when I take my clients back."*

Maggie's instincts had been totally right; the owner of Blooms had faked his way brilliantly through everything. He hired very talented florists to do ALL of his dirty work, because he was totally useless. The guy couldn't even construct a simple corsage, never mind a skillful and dramatic arrangement. That same day, Jackie handed in her floral scissors and went to work for "S."

Mary followed two weeks later. I'm pleased to report that Maggie and Mary are now being paid what they're worth and they are rightfully getting their own time in the sun, as floral designers to the stars!

Adriana's Notorious P.I.G.

"There is a special place in hell for women who do not help other women." - Madeleine K. Albright

For years, Adriana and her colleagues have referred to their boss, a mid-sized communications company owner named Gabe, as "Notorious P.I.G." He's a classic boar of a male boss, and the worst person to work for if you're a young woman, trying to find your footing in a male-dominated industry.

Once, while on a business trip, Gabe had the nerve to ask Adriana if she would ever consider sleeping with a superior, to move up the corporate ladder. It was not an innocent question posed after one too many martinis in the hotel lobby bar, nor even a hopeful hint. It was a warning. She'd seen it many times before - Gabe would book business trips with female interns and young female associate sales reps, then pull the same stunt, time after time. Sometimes the young women would reluctantly go for it, only to realize they'd been duped, and were most definitely not being promoted. Other times, women would just look for other jobs and quietly leave - too nervous and ashamed, to complain to human resources about the owner of the company.

When Gabe propositioned Adriana, literally moments after arriving at their hotel, she was tipsy and jetlagged. She'd had a few glasses of cheap chardonnay on the flight to their Caribbean office, to calm her fear-of-flying nerves. This situation was nothing new. Gabe had tried his hand(s) with Adriana before, but she never gave in. She'd usually just laugh off his advances or ignore him altogether. This time, however, she had liquid courage, and she'd been practising a "F-you" speech for as long as she could remember. Adriana had also been interviewing for jobs with other companies, and she finally had an offer on the table, so she decided to let him have it: *"I heard about the hookers and eight ball of coke in Vegas, Gabe —*

could you be more cliché?" Stunned, he warned her that she'd better know her place if she expected to keep her job.

Unfazed, Adriana told Gabe that he'd earned himself quite the reputation and not just with his employees: *"The communications world is tiny, Gabe,"* she said. *"Everyone knows about your shady business practices, including tax evasion and being sued by multiple suppliers. Bill* (the company's CFO) *told me about your five-hundred-dollar bottle of scotch purchases, and the extensive renos to your home - all with company money. What exactly do you think I have to lose by telling you any of this? You're a jerk. Your managers haven't had bonuses in years, but you don't bat an eyelash over giving yourself huge pay increases every year. EVERYONE knows what's going on!"*

Looking at the completely dumbfounded Gabe straight in the eye, Adriana told him that if he dared try to fire her or abuse any other women in the office again, she would share everything about his deplorable behaviour with his wife, Alexis.

Immediately after that mostly one-way exchange, Adriana ran to the hotel lobby's washroom and threw up. She then crawled to her room and passed out. The next day, she was mortified, unfortunately remembering every single word she had said to Gabe. She was sure she no longer had a job, and she was already planning her return home in her mind. However, it turns out that her not-so-little speech worked. Gabe was as quiet as a mouse for the rest of the trip, and from there on out, he became a complete professional around her and the other women in the office. In fact, Gabe's behaviour had improved so drastically, that Adriana decided to decline her job offer, and stay with the company. Of course, her female colleagues were thrilled with her decision to stay.

11

THE TEENAGE DAUGHTER YEARS

"When the shit hits the fan, useless men hit the road" – Ellie Russo

Julia (Jules)

In all agonizing seriousness, recalling this particular time in my parenting life is a tough one for me. This was the time when my firstborn daughter was a teenager. Although she was gorgeous, smart, and creative, she was also, a parent's worst nightmare. I'll start by saying, God, I love that kid. She's my first girl, and she will always be my sweet baby "Toots," but at the time, she was the wildest 15-year-old girl I've ever known (or heard of). Ever. Even by the end of my university years, I hadn't pulled a tenth of the shit she did on a weekly basis.

This is an old story now – but I had to stop writing this book for quite a while, and come back to it, when I was feeling less down, and more creative. I think I must have been traumatized by the chaos that was my home life, and I believe that I was also fearful that I would damage a pending legal cases against my daughter, at the time, by even talking about her criminal antics.

Truth be told, time does heal almost everything. I barely remember the sleepless nights I spent looking for her when she ran away from home, the drugs that she brought into my home and sold from my home, the bad (bad) boys she surrounded herself with, the daily police visits, and the endless attempts I made to get her the professional help that she needed.

The one thing that has not healed with time, is my colossal disappointment in her father. I often asked myself, *"Where the heck was her dad when she (and I) needed him the most?"* Oh wait, I remember! There he was, next to The Road Runner, with his head buried deep in the sand, scrounging for ACME snacks, and the quickest way out of his parental responsibilities.

If you recall, "ex" Number 1's nickname is Teffy (short for Teflon - because nothing sticks to him). You know where I'm going with this. He loved his daughter as much as I did, and I'm sure at the time, he wanted her to be a happy, healthy, and productive member of society. However, the only way that this was going to happen, was if a street gang called "Society" sprouted up in my middle-class suburban neighbourhood and made her a member. Whenever I asked Teffy for help with Julia, his answer was always the same: *"It's not my problem."* So, I eventually just stopped asking.

While all of this chaos was happening, I was desperate for some good advice. I asked every parent I knew (and didn't know) for some guidance. A useless dad of a kid at Julia's high school (where she'd managed to miss 58 days in a row), bestowed on me some of his parenting wisdom, telling me that the best way to cope with the teenage daughter years is to accept the fact that *"Horrible aliens take our daughters away when they're about 13 and return them to us as regular humans, between the ages of 18 and 20."* What a load of crap, I thought. I remembered my own childhood quite clearly, and if I had done any of the shit that my kid did, my Italian, Irish father would have made good corporal punishment use of a giant wooden pasta spoon.

As a kid, I instinctively knew my place. Although My upbringing may have resembled one long lackadaisical *Married With*

Children episode (to outsiders), when it came to dealing with misbehaving children, my dad could be scary. Me and my siblings knew to keep our noses clean, or at least pretend to, for fear of the spoon (or the belt). And, because my little brothers had me and my sister to pick up their significant slack, their male laziness, always seemed to get a pass.

These days, you most certainly can't hit your kids. Heck, you can't even yell at them, because they know ALL about their protection rights, and will happily quote legislation. By contrast, as a parent, sticking one's head in the sand, doesn't help much either.

Eventually, my then 15-year-old daughter was admitted into a long-term residential "school" for kids with substance abuse and behavioural issues. The car ride to drop her off was something else too. Her father and I were instructed to drop her at a meeting point off the highway. We took two cars, of course. When a white van pulled up to take our daughter away, she flipped me the bird, and her parting words were, *"I hate you."* As difficult as that was to hear, I was relieved that I'd finally get the support of others in my pursuit of her happiness.

When Jules was away, I felt for the first time, in a long time, that I could finally breathe, and I believed that my 3 to 5-year parental prison sentence, at the hands of a terrorizing teen, would be reduced by 12 months – the length of Jules's residential treatment program. As it turns out, my sweet Jules was a tough nut to crack, even for the professionals. She stayed in her program for nearly 2 full years, and in that time, we were able to rebuild our relationship and discover great love, and admiration for one another.

One week before Julia was due to graduate from her program, we (she, I, and her father) had to sign a contract with the school that would hold us all accountable for her ongoing, outpatient treatment. We were given explicit instructions, that for the sake of her stability and well-being, it would be best if she lived with just one parent, full-time, rather than doing the typical "back and forth" between households.

We mutually agreed that Jules should live with her father for a while and finish high school in his neighbourhood. Although she could stay at my place on weekends, the temptation of running into her old crowd at school, and possibly falling into old patterns again, was just too risky. This plan made good sense for everyone. She'd continue to have a solid routine, and I would still get to see her several times a week. As we were all agreeable to this decision, signing the contract was the easy part.

That is… until the day before her graduation ceremony.

As I was prettying up my place, getting it ready for when Julia would be back, and able to spend time with me and her younger siblings, I got a knock on the door. When I opened it, I was served with a document from Teffy's legal firm, informing me that he was asking for sole custody of Julia and Hank, and that he would be suing me for child support.

The short story here is… that time in my life was gut-wrenching. I had already gone into crippling debt (eventually selling my house and becoming a renter), to pay for Julia's extensive bills for her 2-year program, and then I had the legal battle of my life, just to remain her mother (on paper). The word "useless" doesn't come close to an apt description of the man whom I shared children with. "Cruel", "heartless", and (pure) "evil," are far more fitting adjectives.

On the day of Julia's graduation, her father and I were expected to give a speech. I was devastated by the latest uphill battle with Teffy, but I never let him, her, or anyone else smell weakness. In fact, Teffy's brutality became fuel for my survival. His speech was a joke, full of fluffy crap like *"I'm so proud of you Jules, keep up the good work."* Mine was a little more heartfelt.

Julia's Graduation from ███████████ - Mom's Speech:

"You know, when my first of three children came into this world with big, bright, and curious eyes, and a full (full) head of thick hair — I was mesmerized. I knew that her future would be marked by glorious milestone moments, and I couldn't wait to share each one with her.

At the time, I certainly didn't picture that her first major graduation ceremony would look like this.

Fast forward from the birth of my beautiful baby girl, to today, and I can say with complete conviction — that while our lives have endured more ups and downs than a terrifying roller coaster — It has been worth the ride, to get to where we are right now.

MY DEAR DAUGHTER JULES, YOU HAVE COME A LONG WAY BABY!

███████, the first (and the one-and-only), I could not be prouder of you than I am today. You have taught me so much about myself - what it is to be a good parent, and what it means to become the role model that you've needed so desperately from the moment you were born. You've also taught me how

to be strong, to dig deep within myself, and to become a fighter for what is right, what is honest, and what is GOOD.

Long before we entered the ▮▮▮▮▮ *Program, I thought I had it all figured out - but as all parents who have stood before me here, we know that kids and parents don't come with user manuals - we must make it up as we go... and, we rarely get it right - the first time out of the gate.*

Over the past (almost) 2 years ▮▮▮ *you have worked harder than any person I know. You have also held me - your mother - to a lofty level of authenticity, commitment to the program, and deep (and often painful) self-reflection. Thank you for your perseverance and thank you for not asking me - the (once), weaker of us all - to take you home. That not asking, in itself, proves to me that you knew in the bottom of your heart that you were in the right place, and that your commitment to 'the slow and steady wins the race' strategy - is what now has you on the winning side of this treacherous pursuit from an immature and troubled teenage girl - to the beautiful, confident, young woman who now stands before us today.*

Over the last 6 months especially, of this uphill climb, I can say with delight that I have enjoyed our new relationship and our powerful and honest communication. I really enjoy you as a person ▮▮▮ *and I hope that you are starting to enjoy me too. And, in recent weeks — things have even started to feel "normal" — or perhaps it's our new version of "normal."*

My only request from you at this point ▮▮▮ *- is that you work with me to keep the dialogue open and honest and that we continue to keep each other accountable — regardless of how much the truth can sometimes hurt. If we can promise each other that - then I know that we have found the cure to what once ailed our shattered mother-daughter relationship and together, with the rest of our modern family - we can reap the benefits of the* ▮▮▮▮▮ *Program — and truly appreciate how it has enriched each of our lives.*

130

I'm almost done sweetheart, and I'm sure you're saying 'phew' - but I wanted to mention - with some irony - that I started writing this little speech on the day that you made your application for the final stage of the program. That day was April 20th ("4 - 20")... an annual date - not so long ago - that I used to cringe over. That day - now my dear, is a day that holds new and wonderful meaning for me.

There's nothing more to say at this point that hasn't already been said - except that I'm certain that this is the first of many wonderful milestones waiting for you, and I can't wait to share in those celebrations with you.

I love you ███ *I have since the moment you were born – and I am so very, very honoured to be your mom.*

xoxo Mom "

Well, that was my speech. I delivered it without one tear. I waited until I got in the car (alone) to let it all out. After the ceremony, there was a celebration planned at the school for the sole graduate that day, Julia. That celebration never happened. While I slipped away to the washroom, Teffy bolted with Julia and Hank for their own celebration. It was at my father's cottage about 35 minutes away. I was somehow left off the guest list. To this day, I have not spoken to Teffy. My father (who I think I mentioned, lives just 4 doors down, on the same street) and I, understandably don't have much of a relationship either. I can live with that.

This is one chapter in my life that I've happily closed, and I'm finally able to write about it again, without completely breaking down. I'm also pleased to share that beautiful, sweet Julia is now a young adult, and she's achieving straight As in her very tough university program. She's happy, she's healthy, and she's thriving.

Now the world had better watch out for this strong, wise, and very useful woman!

Ella ("Goo")

Well, my "Goo" grew up. Ella's a big girl now... all 15-know-it-all years of her. She's in her second year of high school and in her third year of living with me full-time. Her dad, Derek, lives about 30 minutes west of our home, in another town, with his now, long-time girlfriend, and her 3 children. Ella barely sees or speaks to Derek these days, and sadly, they both seem to like it that way. I have given up trying to facilitate a healthy daddy-daughter relationship, as I've realized he needs to step up to the proverbial plate or continue to strike out.

For a bit of history, things were relatively good between Ella and Derek, until she turned 11. That's when she started to get a voice of her own. Like her sister, Julia, Ella is very tall, honey-haired, and strikingly beautiful, and she's also completely self-absorbed and oblivious to her mother's (or anyone else's) struggles. But unlike her sister Jules, Ella is as typical as any other Instagram posting, Snap Chatting, TikTok-loving, self-loathing teen on the planet. On a positive note, there are no drugs (that I know of), no police visits, no real problems at school (other than she is a mediocre student at best), and no relationship troubles (yet). However, her father will have none of this new Ella. It is, and it always has been, Derek's way or the highway.

When Ella was about 3 years old, Derek, decided that 'his' daughter's path in life, was to become a professional tennis star. For about 11 years, she spent more time on the tennis court, than at home, and she began feeling increasingly isolated. Ella had become *"All work and no play"* – just the way Derek liked it. Derek and I fought constantly about my (and Ella's) belief, that she had a right to a 'normal' childhood, outside of tennis. It's not that I didn't support the tennis thing, because I certainly did. For a long time, it greatly contributed to her mental health and physical well-being. It helped with her severe shyness, and she had become a fantastic athlete. During those years, I happily attended every practice (6 to 7 days a week), and every tournament (2 to 3 times per month).

When Ella started winning (big time), Derek put more and more pressure on her. She became filled with anxiety. She started feeling sick to her stomach, she started sucking on the ends of her long hair, she bit her fingernails, and she developed an ulcer. This was not healthy, and she told him so. As a result, they started fighting constantly. She was becoming a young woman and she was fighting for the right to be one. She got her period, she developed an interest in friends outside of the tennis world, and she wanted a bit of freedom. That's it. She conveyed that she would happily keep playing competitive tennis if Derek was willing to give just a little, and just let her be a kid.

Again, Derek would have none of it. On Ella's 12th birthday, I dropped her off to her father's place. She, I, her sister, and her cousin, had just spent a fun-filled girls' weekend away (from tennis and her father's mounting pressure), and she agreed to share a bit of her time, by celebrating her big day with her dad, and her grandparents. As I was about to drop her off at her dad's home, she started crying. She became fidgety and she suddenly felt sick to her stomach. I made her get out of my car anyway, assuring her it would be a great day – just like the previous two had been. Boy was I wrong.

Apparently, Derek had plans for Ella that didn't include a birthday celebration at all. He booked an all-day court for her. She'd "wasted" two days on having fun with her mom, sister, and cousin, instead of playing tennis like she should have been, and he was going to ensure she made up the time, practising. On the car ride to the court, Ella had a meltdown. She didn't want to play tennis anymore. She hated tennis. Derek (the man-child) had a full-blown temper tantrum while driving. He started screaming at her, calling her horrible names, and pounding his fist on the dashboard. He began driving erratically, and he even threatened to drive the car off a bridge. Ella secretly filmed the whole episode, and she sent it to me.

I watched the clip in horror, then I drove straight to the tennis court, grabbed 'my' daughter, and informed Derek that Ella would no longer be in his care until he got the serious help that he needed. Sadly, Derek refused to get help, and Ella wanted nothing to do with him.

Naturally, Ella was traumatized by the incident and wanted to quit playing tennis entirely. She kept going for a while (under my care), but sadly, she lost any passion she'd once had for the game. Today, I can't even get her to pick up a racquet, or the phone, to call her dad. It's a sad (sad) situation all around, but at least she's living a relatively normal teenage girl's life now.

12

TWENTY- FIVE YEARS TO DEAD — THE ART OF LONG-LASTING MARRIAGE

"The poor wish to be rich, the rich wish to be happy, the single wish to be married, and the married wish to be dead" — Ann Landers

It's funny (or just plain odd), but when I write, eat, clean the house, cook, or do just about any other thing with a television within range, I need to have it on. On the one hand, I think it's because growing up, the TV was ALWAYS on in my house. On the other, I think it's just in my blood. My grandparents owned movie theatres in our hometown, so my family saw just about everything playing on the big screen, the moment it was released. And when we were not at the theatre, we put some serious mileage on our "VCR." You get bonus points if you know what that is ☺.

Growing up as a member of a large family, there wasn't much extra money for expensive trips or excursions. Rather, all of our family outings involved going to the movie theatre. Friday nights were a real treat, that included dinner at Nino's Pizzeria, followed by the third or fourth cinema movie of the week. As my siblings and I got older, we started bringing our friends, and then our dates to the theatre too. We were (not so strangely) very popular – and we were always watching!

To this day, all of my adult family members are movie and TV show freaks. Every big family gathering is always about who can outshine whom with useless movie trivia like, *"What was Fredo's real name in The Godfather, and who was he engaged to off-screen, during filming?"* The further back that one can reach into the movie trivia archives, the better.

I firmly believe that my 'TV-itis' is related to my childhood. My kids, however, are convinced that I just have severe ADHD, and that I need TV as a constant distraction from the chaos going on in my head. They could be right, but I've explained to them that when I was a kid, ADHD and other disorders were considered (by our parents) excuses for not getting good grades in school or keeping our rooms tidy. My eldest and youngest daughters have been diagnosed with ADHD, and I've considered borrowing some of their meds to see if it helps. Then I start thinking about the fact that ADHD meds are a form of speed and I'm already anxious and twitchy enough, then I Google the effects of unprescribed children's medication on adults, and then I make the sound and healthy decision not to take them.

So, where was I? Oh yes, as I'm writing this, I'm watching - well, listening to some lame(ish) old romantic comedy starring Paul Rudd, Reese Witherspoon, one of the Wilson brothers, and Jack. It was quietly playing in the background like Beethoven's Ninth until I heard this incredible line, or a part of it anyway, beautifully delivered by the one and only, Jack Nicholson: *"Twenty-five years to dead."* Can't you just imagine his gruff, and sarcastic delivery now… *"Twenty-five years* (long pause) *to dead."* I don't have the full context of the statement, but I can only rationally assume that it has something to do with marriage, real marriage - you know, the one where they honour the "till death do us part" thing. I, of course, would know nothing about that. I'm a quitter after all. Twice so far, in fact.

However, this fantastic line did make me start to think about the concept of a long-lasting marriage and the incredible sacrifice and patience a woman must have to proudly declare, *"It's our golden anniversary."* After a quarter century together, "golden" doesn't seem adequate for the time served with just one person. A big old bucket of sapphires or diamonds is about the only reward I can think of, that might incentivize me to stick around for twenty-five-plus years!

I'm racking my brain right now trying to think of 'material.' Material, in the sense of knowing and being able to write about couples who have been married for a loooong time. I have a few friends who are getting up there (twenty years, twenty-two years), but they don't air much of their shit, if you know what I mean. For this reason, I don't have much material to put on the page. It seems that only after divorce, do you really get the full story. And even then, it's usually only the woman's version of the story that we get to hear - which, of course, is the real story.

Okay, I have one... My Aunt "Mickey" (Marxine, named after Karl Marx, if that tells you how old she would be if she hadn't died of old age more than thirty years ago) and my dear, sweet Uncle Gord, were married forever. They are the only true example I can think of when it comes to a long-lasting, and incredibly happy marriage. They weren't my biological aunt or uncle, but they were my grandparents' amazing best friends, and they treated us like their own. They were rich old socialites too (so were my grandparents, but sadly their good fortune skipped my generation), and maybe that's why they were so damned happy. Money buys happiness, people. It does, I tell you!

So, Aunt Mickey and Uncle Gord, who did not have children of their own, used to take my siblings and I to fancy country clubs and let us order fancy alcohol-free cocktails, like Shirley Temples and virgin Pina Coladas *"till the cows come home"* (their words, not mine).

They also hosted us for week-long vacations in their Boca Raton, Florida winter home, and they never, ever, ever, ever forgot our birthdays (sorry, teenagers in the house - didn't mean to go all Taylor Swift on you, but then again, here's my ADHD running amuck).

As I now reminisce about the days of old, as in hanging' with the old and rich set, it occurs to me that there is a formula for true betrothed joyousness: Endless piles of cash + no children (except occasionally on loan from other parents) = true marital bliss! OMG, there's no question in my very clear mind now. I, too, could have been happy *"till death do us part"* with just about anyone, if I had boatloads of cash, and only myself to blow it on.

Now I've started to think about Jay-Z and Beyonce. Why did they have to go and kill the dream? They had to go and have kids. Why? Sorry, the channel's been flipped to a Beyonce concert, and there goes my focus once again.

The (Not So) Classic Hollywood Marriage

As rare as it is to know couples who have been happily married for over 25 years, in Hollywood, these types of unions are as unique as finding a needle in a haystack. However, being the movie buff that I am, and a long-time and loyal subscriber to People magazine, I have been able to quickly draw on my repository of useless celebrity knowledge, to come up with a few happy couples, off the top of my head.

In compiling my short list of long-lasting couples, I recalled that Meryl Streep and her sculptor husband, Don Gummer, have been happily married for over 45 years. Then there's Will and Jada Pinkett-Smith, who have been together for more than 25 years, despite a few recent and very public setbacks… But what doesn't kill us, makes us stronger – right?

When I tried to find other celebrity couples to add to my list, my Google search revealed that Meryl & Don, as well as Will & Jada, are no longer together. And despite their deceiving hand-holding trips down the red carpets of Hollywood, these couples have been living apart for many years, but just pretending to be happy couples, for the public, while posing for the paparazzi.

I think it's safe to assume that I know nothing about Hollywood marriages. And, even if I dig my heels in, and try to sell the unshakeable matrimonial devotion between Tom Hanks & Rita Wilson, Sarah Jessica Parker & Mathew Broderick, and even Denzel Washington & Pauletta Pearson, I need to remember that these people are all great actors. So being the "players" that they are, they too, could have us all fooled!

13

EVEN ON THE BIG SCREEN, MEN ARE USELESS

"The useless men are those who never change with the years"
— James M. Barrie

Whether you're watching cinematic masterpieces like *Goodfellas*, *Pulp Fiction*, or *Shawshank Redemption*, or enjoying guilty pleasures like *Pretty Woman*, *Twilight*, or anything starring Sandra Bullock, movies have the magical power to transport us to another time and place.

These timeless classics (and some not-so-timeless) are readily available on our streaming networks, or on our shelves, if we still own DVDs, and they are forever playing in our hearts and our memories. Of the literally millions of movies that have been made since the first, called *Garden Scene*, in 1888, men (and women) have been entertaining us with their good traits like humour, compassion and intelligence, as well as their dishonourable attributes like cringy arrogance, excessive greed, and their violent and criminal ways.

While I have great love for all genres, my own guilty movie-watching pleasure comes from mindless movies. Most of these films feature... you guessed it, useless men! And trust me, I'm far from alone. Some of the top-grossing movies of all time, feature ridiculous and useless idiots, and they are hardly the stuff of cinematic genius. However, these flicks, which let us mentally check out for a few hours and forget about our troubles, are worth the price of the exorbitant movie popcorn. Everyone seeks balance in their lives, and sometimes a light-hearted, useless man movie, can be just the cure. Following are some of my top 'pic' picks:

Three Men and a Baby. Doesn't the title just say it all? Hollywood tapped into the useless man thing ages ago. In reviewing this popular 80s film, you need to consider its 3 stars and just ask *"Why?"* Was the paycheck so great for these super manly men - Tom Selleck, Steve Guttenberg, and Ted Danson, that they'd lower themselves to complete and utter uselessness, just for the sake of a few cheap laughs? Remember Magnum PI? That dude could do anything, and I mean anything (he had previously served as a Navy Lieutenant before becoming a gun-wielding Private Eye), but in this sweet little emasculating movie, he somehow needed the help of his two buddies to change a diaper and heat up a bottle. Really?

The Hangover (or Three Men and a Baby part deux) is another beauty! When this movie was released, about half an hour into the flick, the guys in the audience were killing themselves with laughter, while the women were sitting on the edge of their seats, wondering when someone - anyone, was going to change the baby's diaper and give him a much-needed, and probably life-saving bottle of formula! Again, useless men on the big screen!

It's a tie! Sometimes, it's possible to enjoy a movie that doesn't have much substance if you can manage to lower your expectations, and just watch it for the sake of passing time. Despite being frivolous, the characters in these movies can be quite charming, providing a sense of pure entertainment that doesn't require much thinking. If you have seen any of my top 10 favourite (dumb) movies, starring complete buffoons, you may have also experienced the joy of indulging in these utterly useless male characters:

1. Navin R. Johnson, in *The Jerk*

2. Harry and Lloyd, in *Dumb and Dumber*

3. Everett, in *'O Brother, Where Art Thou*

4. Derek Zoolander, in *Zoolander*

5. Cousin Eddie, in *National Lampoon's Christmas Vacation*

6. Brennan and Dale, in *Step Brothers*

7. Brick Tamland, in *Anchorman*

8. Lt. Frank Drebin, in *The Naked Gun*

9. Borat Sagdiyev, in *Borat*

10. Adam Sandler, in (almost) everything

And finally, there's the movie, ***The Kids Are All Right***. Again, doesn't the movie just say it all? In summary, this is a sweet little story about a lesbian couple, raising several kids together, without men, and you know what? Surprise! Everyone turns out all right!

14

POST-DIVORCE DATING

"Dating after kids and divorce is like dating in high school, only with stretch marks and debt." – Author Unknown

About a year after my second divorce, I decided to give it the ol' college try once again and start "speed" dating. This was not the scenario where you spend 30 minutes, wearing a *"Hello my name is..."* sticker, in an overly air-conditioned conference room, moving from table to table, trying to make a true romantic connection with one of 15 random strangers, in 2 minutes or less. My type of speed dating was taking any, and all men up on their offers for drinks or dinner - to rapidly test out our chemistry and compatibility.

By this time, I was almost over the bitterness of my second failure in the big love department, and I figured, *"What the heck, a girl's gotta' eat"*– right? I planned to say "yes" to every invitation for a date and to give myself a real chance at true love. At the end of what turned out to be a not-so-speedy dating experience (that lasted a couple of years in total), I wound up predictably single again, and less wise than before. Some men stuck around for a while, some relationships were short-lived and nothing but trouble, and the one good guy that maybe I should have hung on to, got away.

Good Guys Want Tough Girls

For about a year, I had one man in my life. He was a good man, a sweet man, a loyal man. He was almost perfect in every way. My man had a fantastic career, he was generous to a fault, and he spoiled me and my kids. On weekends when I was kid-less, he would whisk me away to five-star resorts and he took me on unforgettable adventures in fun and picturesque places like Quebec City, New York City, and Miami. When we stayed in, he cooked like a chef, he cleaned, and he even did the laundry. He also lived in another city. His home was about a 90-minute drive away, and although he was devoted, he also appreciated the geography between us.

"Patrick" (as I'll call him from here on out) was as close to being the perfect man, as a man can get. He had the potential to be my Gord to his Mickey, in as much as he would be "that guy" if it were just the two of us, happily cruising through life in his convertible BMW, without my three kids. No, make that my two kids - specifically the girls. Patrick and Hank? They became as thick as thieves (My ADHD has me Googling if that term is socially acceptable, then I remembered there were several movies by the same title, and I'm all good again).

Hank and Patrick went to the arcade together, they enjoyed go-carting, and they even fine-dined together. As for the girls... ah, the girls. They drove him friggin' nuts. The eldest had been nothing but trouble for a while, as you know, and the youngest was needy beyond even my wildest dreams. That, and the fact that she slept with me every single night, didn't help our desire to satisfy our desires, if you know what I'm saying.

By all accounts, Pat was a great boyfriend. He didn't complain much, but sometimes, he said nothing at all, and his silence was deafening. Our fights, though rare, were always about the girls - and his offering of heartfelt, thoughtful, and ahem, "expert advice" on how I should deal with my daughters' troubling behaviour, was starting to wear on me. He told me that I needed to get tough. I was apparently too soft, and the girls were dragging me down. When he wasn't giving me the silent treatment, he was giving me a lot of *"You know what I would do if I were you..."* guidance.

While all of this wonderful and constructive advice should have been taken as such, it was just too darn hard to sit silently and take it in, while inside my head I was shouting, *"Are you f'king kidding me? How dare you tell me how I should handle my kids? I'm a great mom, and what the hell do you know? You don't live here, you don't have kids, and hell, you've never even lived with a woman, or even had a roommate!"* No, when things went upside down around my place with the slightest kid drama, Patrick immediately scooted away to his luxury bachelor pad many miles away, and he got to leave my everyday hell behind him. When this happened (time and time again), I thought of the old adage, *'When the going gets tough, the tough get going.'*

In a text message from me to Mr. Perfect, just before our third and final breakup in a year, I asked him what would make him happy, and I told him to be honest. Honesty isn't always the best policy, as it turns out. He told me that he loved me very much, but he would love me even more if I learned to be a better parent and was tougher on my children. That hurt, but it was all I needed to reply, *"Well I guess it's time for you to get going tough guy,"* before finally closing this post-divorce dating chapter.

Time To Moving On, Not In

I was out for drinks with my friend Kylie one night. It was the first time I'd gone out, in the several months since my breakup with

Patrick. The place that we picked was packed with trendy men in boy's ball caps, expensive sneakers, and rolled-up jeans. It wasn't really my scene, but in all honesty, I wasn't sure what my scene was anymore.

When Kylie saddled up to the long and rustic bar that was three-deep with ball cap "boys," she knew it would be next to impossible to score us a drink, unless the scruffy barman was able to see her over the sea of hats and catch a glimpse of Kylie's beautiful face. That's when Ethan came to the rescue. Standing beside Kylie, he was very tall, super cute, and he had great dating "game." Ethan casually leaned over to her and asked what she wanted to drink. She told him she wanted two vodka and sodas for herself and a friend. In an instant, Ethan was able to flag the attention of his buddy behind the bar and order our drinks.

Kylie had been single by this point for nearly 5 months, having kicked her useless hipster dude to the curb for not one, but a whopping five indiscretions (that she knew of), throughout their tumultuous nine-month relationship. She was indeed in need of a little attention, and she clung to every word from Ethan's beautiful full lips. His ability to get a drink in her hand in under two minutes flat didn't hurt either.

As the night went on, the two shared many drinks and superficial stories about their amplified careers, exaggerated personal and professional connections, and numerous sexual escapades. It was a match made in short-term lust heaven.

After about an hour of sitting on the sidelines of this lust fest, I was feeling justifiably ignored, so I left. I was excited to get the hell out of there and go home to watch a movie in my comfy (childless) bed, without having to share my family-sized bag of Miss Vickie's salt and vinegar chips. Before I left, I tried to persuade Kylie to come with me, but she refused. She said she'd *"leave after this drink."* She only lived a short walk from the hipster bar, and she promised to text me when she got home.

When I stepped out of the bar, that's when Dayton (Day) stepped in. Day was a nice guy. He was Ethan's best friend and by all accounts, he was a bit of a "cock blocker," as Kylie soon learned. It's not that he was all that interested in Kylie (a gorgeous petite blond with a body like Kim Kardashian's), but he could see that her naive hopefulness with Ethan would lead to nothing but trouble for them both. Ethan was engaged as it turned out, and about to be married to a lovely and sensible girl, and Day knew that Kylie would be but a mere notch on Ethan's soon-to-be wedded bedpost. *"One more for the road"* had recently become Ethan's motto on every fiancée-less evening out with the boys, leading up to his nuptials. And his motto had more to do with women, than wine.

Day had decided he had to put a stop to it, not just for Kylie's sake, but for the honour of Ethan's fiancée. That night, as the bar was about to close, Ethan went to the washroom, and Day took the opportunity to grab Kylie by the hand and lead her out of the bar, and to his car. By this point, she was stumbling but still flirtatious, almost not noticing that it was Day's hand she was holding instead of Ethan's. By the time Day was able to determine where she lived and to get her there in one piece, Kylie had already unbuttoned her blouse, and her hand was on Day's package, in the front seat of his car.

Being the good guy that he was, and not wanting to get a call from authorities for taking advantage of a drunken stranger, Day played it smart and walked Kylie to her door, then left. A few weeks later, Day and Ethan were out at their usual watering hole and began discussing the beautiful, busty blond from their recent past. Day asked Ethan for her number, which he still had, but reluctantly gave up.

Day took the exchange as a good sign that the almost-married boy had accepted his fate as an almost-married man and was about to become an honourable guy. When Day called Kylie to ask if she wanted to hang out sometime, she eagerly said, "Sure, *why don't you come join my friend Ellie and me at a bar on Front Street tonight? Ellie is writing a book about online dating, and she's meeting some dude she has a date with there. I'm just going along for the ride, and you can be my date if you want.*" Day was game.

When Day entered the bar, he immediately sensed trouble. After kissing a sober and well-put-together Kylie on the cheek, he turned to meet Ellie (Moi). Bam! It hit us both between the eyes. Chemistry was now more than just a class I'd failed in high school - it was a feeling neither I, nor he (so he lied), had ever felt so instantly before.

Suddenly, the six-foot-six, ultra-nerdy, online dating dude, that I was committed to for the evening, seemed even less interesting. However, I gave the guy a shot - at least for a little while. After turning my back on Kylie and Day, I leaned into a very dull conversation with the nerdy chemical engineer, but in my mind, I was totally tuned out. Feigning interest, I downed a vodka and soda, and managed to keep my eyes focused on him and his ill-fitting shirt and 90s hairstyle. When Aidan (I think that was his name) suggested we meet up with some of his friends at the bar next door, I was all over it. I thought, *"Maybe he has cool friends and I'll dig him more."*

As soon as we got to the equally lame bar next door, with Kylie and Day in tow, I realized I couldn't take it or fake it anymore. My personality was too verbose, I was too selfish, and I was also way too sober, to put in any more time with the dorky engineer. So, I did what any coward would do. I bolted out the front door without a word to Aidan, who had turned his back on me for a mere 30 seconds, to greet his equally geeky friends. I was a bad person, but at least I was free from another useless and uneventful date with a stranger.

I was relieved when Day and Kylie caught up to me about two minutes after my sneaky getaway. Kylie was laughing, Day... not so much. He scolded me for being cold and heartless, before leading us to some cool underground club around the corner from Loserville. His ability to whisk us past the substantial lineup of twenty-somethings, and into the club was impressive, and that chemistry thing between us was acting up again. His tall hot bod, cool threads, and wicked salt-n-pepper Mad Men hairstyle were driving me wild. His very harsh teasing of me for being a man-eater, also made me want him more. I needed a distraction. After another drink, I set my sights on a hot Latin guy - "*A cool conquest,*" I thought to myself, as I launched my body onto the dance floor, and into his arms.

It was time I shook off these foreign feelings of longing for someone that my sweet and vulnerable friend Kylie may actually benefit from knowing. That's why I turned my attention to someone that I had no real interest in, who could be some innocent fun for a night. Cock Blocker Day had different plans, however. After watching me kiss the hot random dude, he sauntered over to us, grabbed me by the hand (Kylie's was in his other), and decided it was time for us to leave, and go someplace quiet for a civilized chat and some normalcy.

I put up no fight at all. I loved his take-charge attitude. As the rest of the evening progressed, it became evident that the feelings I had for this guy were not going to dissolve into another vodka soda, and I had to face my fears – the fear of hurting my friend, fear of rejection, and most of all, the fear of feeling something I hadn't allowed myself to feel in a really long time.

Very quickly, Day and I became a real couple. Kylie, to my delight, was totally cool with us, too. She started dating a sweet man, and this one seemed to have little to no baggage, for a change. I was happy when I learned that my children wouldn't be an issue between Day and I, as he also had a beautiful little daughter around Goo's age. Things were finally falling into place. Day's little family, complimented mine, and all was as it should be… for a while anyway.

As the months went on, and my blinders came off, I started noticing some particularly disturbing, and invasive facets of Day's personality. My friend Anna was the first to point out his premature "We" affliction. When Anna was at MY house one day for a barbeque, she asked me if I had any hot sauce for her steak. Day, being the gentleman that he was, rose from his patio chair to go inside and fetch the sauce. As he walked away, he said, *"Honey, where do we keep our hot sauce?"* After answering him, I looked at Anna, who shot me her best 'Mr. Spock' look - you know, the one perfect raised eyebrow that says, *"Now, that's a little too familiar, don't you think?"*

After that night, I started to notice a lot of "We" and "Ours" as in *"We should think about moving to the east end of the city"* and *"Our girls will love going to the same school."* It's important to point out that I lived in the west end, where my three kids were firmly rooted, and attending three different schools in our neighbourhood, at the time.

Day lived in the east end, and he only had his daughter with him every second weekend. Even when he met my mother for the first time (we went for a visit, which he insisted on, to her home about two hours north of Toronto, with his daughter and my youngest), his insistence that his child call my mom "Amma" (my kids' name for their grandmother), and his brazen familiarity to call my mother "Mom," truly creeped me (and my mother) out. His pressure to move the relationship at lightning speed became overwhelming. My eldest was starting to get into real trouble during that period and Day decided to take on the role of tough-loving dad, despite my very firm instructions to *"Keep out of it!"*

From then on, my relationship with Day took a downward spiral very quickly. My eldest daughter Julia despised him and called him every name in the book, every chance she got. She also threatened me with an ultimatum, *"Him or me, Mom!"* With that, I knew that I needed to get some healthy distance from him, fast, if there was ever a chance at giving my daughter some security in our paper-thin mother-daughter relationship. The more I started to push back and ask for some space from the guy, hoping to return to a more casual and fun dating relationship, the more he pushed for a commitment. He even talked about moving into MY house with his daughter (I later found out that I would have been the fourth woman whose home he'd moved into, if I had allowed it).

At that point, I knew this guy was what Vince Vaughn would refer to as a *"Stage Five Clinger,"* in the movie *Wedding Crashers*. Too much too soon, and because my troubled teen despised the guy (and quite honestly, I was starting to a well), I had to cut him loose.

15

YOUNG LOVES

"Age is just a number. It's totally irrelevant unless, of course, you happen to be a bottle of wine." – Joan Collins

My "Beau"

As I continued playing the dating game, I learned a valuable lesson. Men are not mouldable – especially when they hit their late 40s and 50s. Women probably aren't either, but at least the art of compromising is in our DNA. The proverbial 'they' say, *"You can't teach an old dog new tricks."* And they are "spot" on. As men age, they get set in their ways and their routines, so the best you can hope for when you settle for an old dog, is to be blessed with cat-like agility to be able to adjust to his schedule. Ahh - no thanks!

While it's not okay to absolve inappropriate male behaviour (i.e., like getting drunk and being disorderly), by just chalking it up to a "Boys will be boys" mindset, there's nothing wrong with the playful side of that phrase. Most young(er) men know how to have some fun, and not take themselves so seriously. However, for many men my age, the free-spirited playfulness of boyhood has long been forgotten, despite the fact that men attempt to remain "young" in other ways.

My experiences with dating men in their mid-life have been mostly disappointing. I found that they often have inflated egos, matched only by their swollen bellies, that are covered up by expensive and too-hip clothing, which only highlights their insecurities. At our age, men should be confident, secure, and subtle,

152

but I've witnessed the opposite. And, after a while, I grew tired of going on date after date with these types, so I decided to take a break from playing the game, at least for a little while.

When my daughter went away to her 2-year rehabilitation school, I could finally breathe. I spent lots of fun and peaceful time with my son and my youngest daughter. We did regular drama-free stuff together. Hiking, apple picking, and road trips were wholesome family times, and carefree fun was suddenly in our lives again. I was also able to enjoy my free time away from my kids – no longer having to worry about the constant state of chaos that surrounded our family.

One night, I went to a Fleetwood Mac concert with my ex-sister-in-law (and still good friend), Tracey. We had a blast. We danced in the aisles with strangers, and we sang every amazing tune the band played, until our voices were raw. And for the first time since I could remember, I did not need to rush home to make sure the house wasn't on fire. With no kids at home and a full free night to have some unadulterated fun, we decided to have a nightcap after the concert, at a bar close to Tracey's place.

That's when I met Beau. He was 20 years younger, and I was gob-smacked and amused that a "boy" would be interested in a middle-aged woman. After a few cocktails and some coaxing on his part, I gave him my number. I'd clearly had no (real) success dating men my own age and I thought "What the heck – have a little fun. This couldn't possibly turn into anything real." To my surprise (and that of my friends and family), we became more than a fling. From Beau's beautiful bee-stung lips, and deep blue eyes to his mischievous smile, I couldn't help but get lost in my infatuation with him.

When our one-night stand, turned into buying a little house together and shacking up for nearly 3 years, I found myself truly, madly, deeply in love, possibly for the first time ever. It was a beautiful thing until it suddenly wasn't. The signs that we wouldn't make it were always there I suppose, but I just chose to ignore them. He was restless, and I was aching to be settled. He was a reckless adventurous type who raced cars, boats, and motorcycles. He was wild and free, and he could sometimes be a very immature "boy" who threw bonafide temper tantrums. Throughout our relationship, I often found myself playing "the fixer" to his many family, friend, and work problems. Simply, I had my blinders on because I loved him.

Crash and burn it did not. It ended subtly and with sadness - more mine than his - but it ended. My Beau was just shy of his 29th birthday, and I had just turned 49. One final trip to Mexico was the beginning of the end. A broken arm (mine) on day 2 of our "romantic" vacation, in an unfortunate scooter incident, kind of sealed the deal. I was nursing my wounds the whole trip, while he was nursing his drinks, and paying attention to everyone but me. For the first time, I was feeling like a third wheel in our duo.

When we returned from that last vacation (accompanied by his sister Em and her much, much older boyfriend, Ron), I knew we were done. This incredible thing had run its course. My boy who was also my man, was no longer in love with me. He was too sweet and classy to cut the cord, so I did it for him. That very same day, Beau grabbed his surfboard, moved out, and caught a plane to Costa Rica, to catch some waves, and a local girl his own age. Within a year, Beau was married, and had a baby. They made plans to move back to

Canada – which felt a little too close for my comfort, but at least I'd had some time to heal, and move on.

That was a few years ago, but he still calls me sometimes, asking for advice about stupid shit – like how to deal with his controlling mother and his *"annoying"* sister. I think he sometimes forgets that I'm no longer his 'fixer.' According to his sister Em (who I am still close with), Beau is angry, unhappy, and drinking far too much these days. Plus, he blames the world for the fact that he now has a kid, big responsibilities, and he can no longer get away with acting like a spoiled child. Being a grown-up is hard - I get it. I've been one for a long, long while, and now I can look back on my relationship with Beau and know that I got the best part of him.

I discussed in an earlier chapter, how time heals all wounds, and I know in my heart that this is true. Time also gives us the gift of great clarity. Case in point... now, when I see Beau's number come up on my phone, I'm certain that he's calling to whine about his perceived terrible life, and not to ask how I'm doing (nor care what my answer might be), so I just roll my eyes, and let his calls go to voicemail.

Alex

After my breakup with Beau, I grew sad, then angry, and then (slightly) bitter. In my mind, we'd spent almost 4 beautiful, connected years together (minus his frequent temper tantrums), and in a heartbeat, he was married and with a child. It felt cold and wrong for me to be so lonely, while he was enjoying new parenthood, and marital bliss with someone he barely knew. That's when I decided to try to recapture those magical feelings that I longed for – with another man, who was much younger, of course.

I met Alex on a dating app – *Hinge* I think. I deliberately avoided hook-up sites like *Tinder* and *POF* (or "Plenty of Fucks," as my friend Bridgette calls it). Quality men, I was told, could only be found on sites like *Bumble, Match.com* and *Hinge*. I later discovered that guys didn't distinguish one dating site from the next, and they just multiplied their chances of scoring, by having profiles on all of them, at the same time.

Despite the terrible odds of finding a good guy, I lucked out anyway. Alex was just my type - tall, dark, and handsome, and to my surprise, he was looking for a serious relationship. Soon, Alex and I were spending a lot of quality time together. He wasn't at all wild and crazy like Beau had been, and he preferred spending nights staying in, making dinners, watching documentaries, and having long, deep conversations, over going to bars and clubs like the rest of the men his age. I really liked spending time with Alex, although our relationship very quickly started resembling that of an old married couple, despite our significant age gap. In other words, we were very (very) boring together!

Sadly, just days before the madness of the COVID-19 pandemic hit, Alex and I were about to embark on our first big trip together – Alex's friend's swanky wedding in Sardinia, Italy. I was excited to get away, and hopefully pry Alex from his conservative shell so that the young man could loosen up and 'live a little.' Expectedly, the wedding was cancelled due to the pandemic. While I was disappointed to be missing the trip of a lifetime, I was also relieved to have escaped certain judgment from the many age-appropriate couples, who I knew would also be at the wedding.

While life was sweet and predictable for a while, albeit boring, Alex eventually started to grind on my nerves. The pandemic was in full force. The world had shut down, and Alex and I were essentially shut in – together! Also, during that time, my elderly mom (who was as equally talkative as Alex) moved in with me and my daughter, to weather the pandemic storm with us. I hadn't lived with a parent since I was 18, and cohabitating with my mother so many years later, was a major adjustment, to say the least.

Alex lived in mid-Toronto, while I was about 40 minutes west, in the suburbs. The lack of traffic at that time, made travelling back and forth between our places, relatively easy for me, although I wish I'd have had somewhere (anywhere) else to go for some lighthearted fun. As Alex was officially part of my pandemic "bubble," along with my mom and my pre-teen daughter, my only outlets for entertainment, included listening to Alex and my mom talk ad nauseam; to me, at me, with each other; against each other, and NON-STOP! Alex was completing his third post-graduate degree at the time, and his latest was a PhD in philosophy. I thought it was kind of a useless degree, and a waste of money, but what did I know – I chose to get a job after 4 years of university, instead of making school my full-time career.

For the almost one year that we were a couple, Alex and I felt monotonous, like an episode of *Suits, Season 9* - on repeat. We made food, watched boring TV shows and documentaries, read books, and discussed everything under the sun, including the meaning of death – until I almost wished for my own. You know, sometimes I just wanted to be left alone to watch mindless episodes of *Bachelor in Paradise* and eat Häagen-Dazs from the container, in silence.

One day when Alex was at my place, droning on about the difference between deductive and inductive arguments in philosophy, I asked him out of curiosity (and annoyance), what he wanted to do (when he grew up), with his extensive education. With a straight face, he told me, *"I think after this, I'll complete at least one more post-grad degree, then I'll probably teach, or be a Philosopher. "*

I burst into explosive and uncontrollable laughter. I think my repressed comic relief for the past year, had been waiting for just the right moment, to push open the floodgates. When I managed to compose myself, I realized that Alex was glaring at me with pure disgust, and I knew there was no turning back, at that point. So, with my own straight face, I said to him, *"Oh that makes sense. I saw a posting on Indeed for an Associate Socrates and another on LinkedIn for Plato's Apprentice."* Again, I couldn't contain myself and bent over in a fit of laughter. When I stood upright, Alex was gone. For good (riddance).

Serra's Married Young Man

"Hell, hath no fury…" Yadda, yadda, yadda - we all know how it goes when you're a woman on the receiving end of a breakup. But what if a scorned woman chose to take her reprisal another way? What if she decided to not be sad or play the victim but to just play the field? That is Serra's story.

It's a fact. Serra's had more relationships than most (women or men). She's a self-proclaimed "serial dater, "a long-term and short-term girl, who is rarely out of one relationship before she's on to the next. Serra claims that she's not proud of her lengthy mating history and she often lies about it to her potential suitors. She says, "*No man wants to imagine that his woman has been with anyone other than him. However, with a failed marriage behind me and 2 kids, I'm pushing it if I try to sell the 'less than 5 bedfellows' tale, that your average smart dating woman peddles. So, I stick with my 'less than 10' story and never commit to an actual number. That way I can look experienced but not too experienced, and my men can imagine that my number is more like 6 or 7. It's a good, solid strategy.*"

After her very messy divorce, Serra "dated" a lot of younger men. She liked the fact that they had no real baggage, and she easily enjoyed their unadulterated time together – no matter how brief. Serra was determined to play the field and not get emotionally attached to one man, as she felt loving someone made her vulnerable, and weak. And she'd had plenty of those feelings during her marriage.

When Serra met Massimo at an airport lounge in Toronto, on her way to New York City for a 3-day business trip, the sparks flew. Massimo was 32 (Serra was 47), and he was a very successful tech entrepreneur. He was also Italian, and forthcoming that he was a married man. Serra didn't care. From the plane ride to New York, Serra and Massimo headed straight to his beautiful hotel room at the Ritz and there, they started their steamy affair. When they parted ways 3 days later, Serra hadn't even laid her head on a pillow in her own hotel room at the Sheraton. The affair was full steam ahead, and the lovers made plans to keep their good thing going.

Massimo was frequently in Toronto and New York for business, and he easily convinced Serra that they could have a beautiful on-again-off-again relationship of convenience. She thought this was ideal, given that she was also not interested in a commitment, and she would have lots of free time to herself.

Predictably, the sexy affair lost steam after a few months. Serra started developing real feelings for "Mass," and she made the mistake of saying the "L" word while on one of their late-night, boozy phone calls. Suddenly Mass's phone calls and trips to North America slowed down, and Serra became desperate. Then she made the ultimate other woman blunder. After two weeks of radio silence, Serra called Massimo's office and spoke to his assistant, under the guise of being a client from Toronto. When she learned that he was in San Francisco for the next few days, she hopped on a plane to California and took an Uber to the Ritz-Carlton (Mass always stayed at The Ritz).

On her way to the front desk, Serra saw Massimo, his beautiful young wife, and his two "mini-me" children, get off the elevator and walk towards the front door of the hotel. Serra and Mass locked eyes, and his icy stare, instantly locked her out of his life – permanently!

All that reality was a tough pill for Serra to swallow. She confessed that it took her a long time to get the vision of Massimo's beautiful young family out of her head, and to forgive herself for the shame she felt for having an affair. After the Massimo incident, Serra vowed to *"never date a married guy again, and to stick to predictable and boring men her own age,"* from then on.

16

MAMA'S BOYS – FACE IT, WE WILL NEVER MEASURE UP!

"Men are what their mothers made them" - Ralph Waldo Emerson

Bella's Bambino

My jogging pal Bella recently told me that her husband Johnny *"has an umbilical cord that stretches all the way to Italy,"* where his beloved mama, Francesca (Fran) lives. We had a good laugh over that until Bella started crying - for real.

Bella and Johnny have been together for eight years. Both are of Italian descent, though each was raised in Canada. Long before Johnny and his thirty-something-at-the-time brother Dom finally moved out of their parent's home in Toronto, their mother Fran decided she'd had enough of life with a controlling husband, two needy sons, and serving these men, day, and night. One morning she woke up before the rest of her family, she packed her bags, purchased a one-way plane ticket to Calabria, Italy, and moved back to her homeland, and away from the useless men in her life.

In the nearly sixteen years since Frances left her men, she's returned to Canada for short visits, although she'd never met Johnny's wife (and my friend) Bella, with whom he has two young kids. There's no denying that Fran prefers to be the main woman in her sons' lives, so she stays with Dom when she visits. At Dom's place, there is a lot of extra room, and there's no girlfriend or wife for Fran to have to share with her youngest son.

Whenever Fran is in town, she summons her eldest, Johnny, every single day, to come and dote on her at Dom's place. You see, in Francesca's time away from her men, she learned a thing or two about putting herself first, and she successfully graduated from primary caregiver to prima donna.

Recently, Fran came for a "short" visit. This time, she decided to let Johnny's other woman in on the whole Fran experience, and she graciously accepted Bella's offer to stay with them while she was in town. Fran originally planned to stay for a month, but this morning, as Bella was telling me her story (very quietly from the basement bathroom), I learned that Fran's been staying with Bella and her family for nearly four months now, and she's given no indication that she'll be leaving anytime soon. *"Why would she go?"* said Bella. *"Frances has everything she could ever want here with Johnny. He buys her favourite magazines, shampoo, chocolates, and even her favourite perfume. For Valentine's Day, John walked in with a huge bouquet of roses and some chocolates for his mother, yet I got squat."*

Through her tears, Bella let it all out; *"When I told John how hurt I was that he is so incredibly attentive to his mom and that I'm starting to feel like a second-class citizen in my own home, he had the nerve to tell me that his mom will always be number one until the day she dies, and I can either like it or lump it."*

As a traditional Canadian Italian wife of a demanding, slightly lazy, and controlling husband, Bella had been well-trained to serve and protect her husband and kids better than the "Po-po." But while she'd been playing the role of a typical Italian wife, she'd also just inherited a no-longer-typical Italian mother-in-law. I wasn't one

162

to really give advice, given my own beaten down wifely track record, but THIS, I couldn't just sit on quietly.

Bella and I met the next day for a jog, then coffee at a local diner. Over the course of our meeting, a few cups of coffee turned into a few glasses of vino for Bella, and I told her that she needed to get the woman out, now! Fran was never going to willingly leave as long as Johnny continued to treat her as the female head of the household. Heck, he even made Bella give up their bedroom and move to the spare, for finicky Fran. With this revelation, I eagerly offered to help Bella write a "Dear Johnny" email to her stupid hubby. In it, she (we) told Johnny that she'd be happy to "lump it" and put up with the *"Prima-Donna-Mama"* for just one more day. But that was it!

With my encouragement, Bella grew a set of cojones and told Johnny that it was either her or Fran, and if he picked Fran, then she and the kids would be gone by sunrise the next day. Well, what do you know? By sunset that same day, Francesca was out of their home, and back to little brother, Dom's.

When I called Bella a few days later for the update, she reported that Fran had left for "home" earlier that morning. Apparently, Dom met the love of his life and she had moved in. Dom's new girlfriend was a French-Canadian woman named Manon, and she put up with absolutely no sh*t from Fran or anyone else. Manon broke it down for Fran, and explained to her that she would be a respectful guest in their home, and she would just have to "like it or lump it" if she wanted to stay. Fran didn't like it, so she left. I heard that the seat on the plane ride back to the homeland was a little lumpy.

And In Other Italian Mama's Boy News...

My friend Mel recently sent me a link to a New York Post article by Snejana Farberov, entitled, *"Big Babies: Italian Mom Wins Court Battle to Evict her 'Parasite' Grown Sons from Home."*

I love this story for all the wrong reasons, but before I share, here's a bit of background first. In Italy, it's common and culturally acceptable for grown children in their 30s to (still) live with their parents. Not surprisingly, the practice of lingering in the family home well into adulthood is especially common among men, who have been mockingly dubbed "Mammoni," or "Mama's Boys." A recent survey found that less than a third of Italian men under the age of 35, have flown the nest.

One Italian mother, however, decided that she'd finally had enough of her sons' mooching madness, and she was determined to do something about it. This 75-year-old (unnamed) retiree and mother, living in the northern city of Pavia, Italy, filed a lawsuit in the Tribunal of Pavia, accusing her sons, ages 40 and 42 of overstaying their welcome. Fed up with her middle-aged sons' freeloading ways, the mother won an epic court case to have the pair of *"parasites"* evicted from her home.

According to details from the court filing, the mother's complaint stated that both grown men, are employed but have continued living in her apartment, rent-free. The mother is separated from her husband (of course) and lives off her modest pension, all of which goes toward home upkeep and food. To make matters worse for the poor woman, the duo of moochers has not been contributing financially, or even helping around the house with chores, the lawsuit claimed. Judge Simona Caterbi sided with the mother, ruling that the sons, whom she mocked as "Bamboccioni," or "Big Babies," had one month to move out of their mother's apartment.

In her decision, Judge Caterbi wrote, *"There is no provision in the legislation which attributes to the adult child the unconditional right to remain in the home exclusively owned by the parents, against their will and by virtue of the family bond alone."*

Armed with this precedent that living at home well into adulthood is considered culturally acceptable, the sons lawyered up and countersued their mother to stop her from evicting them, arguing that Italian parents are obligated by law to *"maintain"* — or support their children as long as needed. In her decision, Judge Caterbi acknowledged the existing law, but she argued *that "It no longer appears justifiable considering the two defendants are subjects over 40, and once a certain age has been exceeded, the child can no longer expect the parents to continue the maintenance obligation beyond limits that are no longer reasonable."* The attorney representing the sons told local news outlets the two sons had not decided yet if they would appeal the eviction order.

Babcia's Boy

Mention the word "moving," and it's enough to make anyone cringe - particularly those who have kids, and therefore, piles of useless stuff. Throw a useless soon-to-be ex-husband into the mix, and the challenge becomes mountainous. When I was divorcing Hubby Number 2, I sold my house (to get him out), and then I had to deal with the giant task of packing up the place, alone. It was a big house with five bedrooms, a living room, a family room, and a furnished basement. Just one month before my next big move, Number 2 finally agreed to vacate the premises, so that I and my 3 children could move back in, and I could get packing.

Derek's move from the matrimonial home was not much of a move at all, though. He took his truck full of junk and dumped it at his Polish mother ("Babcia," to my kids) and father's home, where once again, he received the royal treatment. This included his mother preparing and serving him *"Three squares a day,"* as he so (not) cleverly liked to brag. The daily menu offered a hot and filling breakfast of sausages, eggs, and pancakes. There was a delicious home-cooked meal for dinner consisting of hearty soup, pierogies, and a variety of delectable meats and cheeses. And every day, Babcia packed Derek a flavourful lunch, complete with his favourite chocolate pudding, to take to work every day. All this free-loading goodness was in addition to having his laundry done, his bed made, and his room cleaned by his devoted mother. What more could a useless son want?

Long story short, when my second marriage crumbled and it was time to move out and onward, I packed up the entire house, including the kids' stuff, as well as my soon-to-be ex-husband's belongings. Derek naturally, couldn't be bothered to help. He was busy luxuriating at his mother's home.

To get rid of all the extra "stuff" we had lying around, I organized a big two-day garage sale. Around 5:00 p.m. on the second day of the sale, Number 2 showed up with a moving van and a crew of his useless guy friends. Within an hour, they were able to load up the remainder of his tacky loot, including hockey and football paraphernalia, a computer, an old stereo, some bad WW2 "art," and clothing. As Derek was finishing up and about to leave, he had the nerve to ask if I could spare him some of my furniture for the new bachelor pad he'd just purchased. Being the generous and beaten-down woman that I was, I relented and told him to take whatever he wanted, meaning some of the furniture that was for sale. I did not mean that he could take half of the profits from the sale of MY stuff. However, the bozo had the audacity to reach into the cash box and help himself to a wad of money, from the sale of my possessions. I don't know why, but somehow, he still seemed able to shock me.

After I gained my balance and watched him drive off towards his mommy's house in his rented U-Haul, I was determined to consider his theft part of the price I had to pay to be rid of the useless fool once again.

Finally, Tara's Time

And speaking of moving . . . there's my friend Tara. Her husband Michael rivals my ex for true uselessness. For some reason, their family of 4 has moved homes three times in the last two years, and all within a ten-kilometre radius. As soon as the roof in one home started to leak, or major repairs were needed, Tara's hubby decided to move to another, rather than fix their place up. Being the doting wife and mom that Tara is, she always went along with her husband's crazy schemes, falling for his repeated claim that, *"Now is a great time to sell."* However, their last move was the "piece de resistance." Tara packed up the entire house while her husband was conveniently "working" on his own business, from the cozy comfort of his mother's house.

Foolishly, Tara never complained when she was alone caring for her *"Tasmanian Devil boys"* (as she affectionately called her sons), all while getting the house in shape to sell and packing up all their non-essential items before the next move. Moving day was the worst, though – it was the stuff of movies, I tell you. When I popped by their home, after my workday to say hi, and to see how things were going, I was aghast to learn that Michael took off just as the movers arrived, making the excuse that his mother needed him (for something), and he had to leave. Sucking it up once again, Tara did what needed to be done - solo. She moved her entire home and her kids, and she got everyone settled in their new place, just down the road. She was exhausted, but then again, she was always exhausted. This was her norm.

A year after the move, as their new home started to show signs of wear and tear at the hands and feet of her wild boys, so did Tara's marriage. One more move was in her near future, but little did Michael know, that this time it would be solo – and not as in "Hans", but as in "Sans," en francais. Michael strangely did not put up much of a fuss when his wife finally left him. Tara thinks he really just wanted to move back home to his mom's place anyway.

With her marriage now a year behind her, and with primary custody of the boys, Tara told me something that made more sense than anything I'd ever heard before. When I asked her how she was feeling about her new life without Mike, she said, *"You know, it's funny, when you no longer have any expectations, disappointment just seems to vanish."* She also told me that he's still "spending quality time" (as Michael calls it) with his parents, yet his mother calls Tara daily, pleading with her to *"Please take him back."*

17

ONLINE DATING – IT JUST "LOL's" ME OUT!

"Can you imagine a world without men? There would be no crime and lots of happy fat women." - Nicole Hollander

When I started writing this book several years ago, I had never been on a dating app. The thought of matching with someone virtually, having awkward conversations, and then meeting up (in a public place of course) to force chemistry, seemed torturous. However, it was also necessary for the sake of "research." Many of my single gal pals had met their significant (for now) others on these sites, so my test subjects were down to little old me, and anyone else I could coax, into helping me dig up some online dating ("OLD") dirt.

At that time, I only really knew about POF, so I jumped into the fishy man-finding tank and decided to give it a whirl. To my surprise, most eligible "gentlemen" taking my bait were, on average, about fifteen years older or fifteen years younger, and most were complete losers (and horny losers at that). It was an eye-opener. It was also refreshing to discover that there were a few handsome and intelligent men out there as well. In fact, after chatting with a few nice, "normal" guys, I decided that if I ever truly had the desire to drop my pride and laundry list of insecurities to go fishing for a man, I would have to put my preconceived notions of online dating aside and test the waters. Here are a few of the fish tales I reeled in along the way:

"LOL"

I have never had much of a presence on social media. I also try to limit my use of texting slang as much as possible, because I think it eventually makes you a very poor communicator, and incapable of stringing a proper sentence together. Take the acronym, "LOL" for example. That's short for "Laugh Out Loud," in case you've been living under a rock for more than a decade. Simply, "LOL" is stupid, and it drives me nuts.

"LOL" is overused (still), and rarely do I receive a text that has me laughing out loud. It's also littered throughout men's dating profiles like punctuation, and in online conversations, it's scarcely omitted. When I first saw "LOL," I thought of Thomas Hayden Church's moronic but loveable character, "Lowell" from the 90s TV show, *Wings* (funny show, "btw"). Therefore, I thought it was some kind of acronym for being a moron. Even now that I know what it stands for, I still think only morons use LOL.

Here are a few real excerpts from some online dating exchanges I enjoyed. I hope they make you "LOL."

Man 1: Hey I like your profile. You seem smart. How goes your Sunday? LOL

Me: Not bad. Thanks for asking. How's your day?

Man 1: Can't complain. Lots of snow out there, eh? LOL. Did you have to shovel?

Me: No. I'm lucky, I live in a condo! How about you - did you have to shovel?

Man 1: Nope, I live in a condo, too, LOL!

Man 2: r u gonna share some more pics? You seem hot, LOL

Me: No - I'm a coward. Besides, you're 16 years younger than I am.

Man 2: I was hoping you could teach me a few things, LOL. I'm totally into Cougs, LOL

Me: As tempting as that offer is, I'm going to have to respectfully decline.

Man 2: Okay, well, let me know if you change your mind. I'll be here, LOL

Following are a few other shining examples of what's out there for us single and sophisticated ladies. These are actual excerpts from male profiles. I did an "advanced search" (because I'm now a pro in the know), and was delighted to discover that hundreds – yes, hundreds of witty gents have used "Laugh Out Loud" as the core of their username (i.e., Laughoutloud007, LOL23, loltilithertz, etc.).

LOL Profile #1: *"Hello there! Where do I begin? I'm a simple man with simple needs and simple demands. I am of a European background and love my culture. I am an old-fashioned type, so I can love, respect, and treat a lady the right way, LOL. I work hard and play harder - when needed, LOL. I am trying this online dating thing in hopes of finding a woman who will love and respect me, as I am not here just for what she wants and needs me to be. I have a very outgoing personality and have a sense of humor, LOL. I tend to be outspoken at times, but that's the culture in me. If you feel there is a possible connection, message me and we'll ride off into the sunset together, LOL"*

LOL Profile #2: *"Thanks for stopping by my place LOL. As you can see I'm an outgoing, funny, laid-back, trustworthy, honest, caring, considerate, kind*

171

guy who is a real GENTLEMAN. If you want a real guy like this and not some of the other posers out there, LOL, then I'd love to get to know you more if I may. I treat my woman as if she were my precious daughter. I want a woman who loves me for me and not possessions like money, cars, etc. I love taking care of my partner, and yes ladies, I do know how to cook (and no, not just microwaving, LOL). I enjoy cuddling. Please ask me if you want to know more. I just don't want to bore you, LOL."

I have to admit, "I treat my woman as if she were my precious daughter," did get a little involuntary 'LOL' from me.

LOL Profile #3: *"I'm a really cheeky guy and sarcastic as hell, LOL. I love taking the piss out of you, but I also love making a girl my queen. My passion is human rights. There's a lot I like to fight for, and I feel everyone should try and make a contribution—no matter how small or "Double D big" it is, get it? LOL. I'm looking for a girl with intelligence but who loves good old-fashioned banter, too. A girl that can talk well is a massive turn-on if you know what I mean, LOL."*

Now this guy was the biggest loser …with a CAPITAL "L"

LOL Profile #4: *"You must NOT have a photo to contact this user! LOL. I'M NOT THE ELEPHANT MAN, JOHN MERRICK. LOL. JUST LOOKIN FOR ONE CERTIFIABLY INSANE WOMAN. I stole this phrase from the one and only episode of South Park I watched. LOL. I HAD A NICE EXPENSIVE SUIT, BUT THE MOTHS ATE IT SO NOW IT'S JUST TEES AND JEANS OR MY B'DAY SUIT. LOL ;-). IF I DATED A JEWISH WOMAN WOULD I HAVE TO REMOVE MY FORESKIN? LOL. THINGS AREN'T ALWAYS AS THEY APPEAR.DON'T ALWAYS BELIEVE WHAT YOU HEAR. I'M NOT SURE IF I'M GOING TO HEAVEN OR HELL. MAYBE SOMEWHERE IN BETWEEN.LOL. I WAS TOLD THIS SITE IS FULL OF REPEAT*

USERS. KIND OF LIKE REPEAT OF-FENDERS.LOL.COITUS INTERUPTUS - IS THAT LATIN? LOL. IMAGINE HAVING FIRST NAMES SUCH AS CUNNILINGUS OR FELLATIO. WAS FELLATIO ALGERNON THE TITLE OF A BOOK? DO WOMEN MASTURBATE MORE FREQUENTLY THAN MEN DO? LOL. SOME WOMEN OF THIS SITE ARE IN DESPERATE NEED OF MAKEOVERS. LOL. DID I ACTUALLY TYPE THAT? HEHEHE."

The only thing the last guy got right was that you'd have to be certifiably insane to meet up with him. And to think, I found those winners in a matter of moments. What a gold mine of material. And then, from seemingly nowhere, just as I was ready to deactivate my bogus profile for good, this truly awesome guy's profile fell into my online net, and not one LOL in his intro:

The "Good Guy" Profile

"My mom used to tell me to never go grocery shopping when I was hungry. I am finding that there are many people here on this site who are shopping while they are "hungry." Why does everyone have to try so hard? Romance is NOT about trying to bring to life some cheesy Hollywood movie. Romance is all about having fun, right from the very first flirtatious exchange. You are coming off as a bit "hungry" when you take desperate measures to create a fairy-tale love story. Let me give you some examples. Online Usernames like "ucompleteme12"(How disappointing that ucompleteme 1-11 were taken), loveu4ever, sadw8ing4u, iwantmysoulm8, and any other usernames containing one of the Disney Princess characters, all seem desperately hungry to me. When it comes to come-ons and propositions, any girl so anxious to have sex with me that she begins correspondence with a sexual proposition and fantasy dirty-talk clearly needs to get "some" before she

contacts me or any other guy. This type of communication is not attractive or sexy. In fact, why not send those emails to the shirtless guys who take pictures of their junk in the bathroom? A big part of the fun of dating is flirting, building chemistry, and really getting to know one another on a deeper level, before engaging in some awesome sex, and then hopefully a beautiful romance together. That's all I am saying. Bring the real you to the party. That's the girl I want to go home with and keep coming home to."

Hmmm, so what's a defiantly anti-online dating kinda single girl to do? Go on a date with this refreshing 'tell it like it is man,' of course - which is exactly what I did. "Magnum," as I'll call this gent from here on out, made the real Magnum PI look like a tiny little boy in person. When we met at a bar, halfway between my house and his (I naturally got there early to down a glass of liquid courage), I was awestruck to see what seven feet and one inch looks like in HD. I'm no slouch at five foot ten and more like six feet two in my permanently well-heeled feet, but holy crap... he was larger than life.

Taken aback, I took a big sip of my glass of Cabernet Sauvignon, deciding that the date would be just that - a date. *"Don't be getting into any cars or beds with this fella if you expect to survive the night,"* I told myself. Magnum sat down on a high stool at one of the bar's bistro tables where I was nervously waiting for him. This mere action of him sitting brought him into the realm of mere mortal, rather than mythological god. When I was finally able to get a good look at his handsome and warm face, instead of his wall of torso, I decided to get to know the guy who wrote that awesome profile. We ordered a drink - his first and my second - and we started to talk like we'd known each other for years. He was very smart, witty, and a total gentleman. I was intrigued. When he walked me to my car, two hours, and a riveting conversation later, he hugged me, and we made plans for a second date later that week.

Many fun dates ensued over the next several weeks, and the banter and the chemistry were off the charts. We put in the time to get to know one another before there was physical intimacy, and we agreed that "waiting" was the right thing to do if there was a chance that this could become the real deal.

The morning after we had sex, I sent Magnum a playful text; *"Thanks for the magical night my prince - ucompleteme13,"* to which he naturally replied *"LOL."* Awesome, right? "LOL" had become our ongoing inside joke, and I was happy that he "got me."

Sadly, as it turns out, I was wrong about this phony too. After that first (and only) magical evening together, I decided to play it cool. I waited for Magnum to make the next move. We'd been texting, talking, and seeing each other regularly for weeks, leading up to our big night, but now I was getting the cold shoulder – which I later learned was called "ghosting." I couldn't believe it. I was a cool chick, decidedly "not hungry," and certainly worth the wait. I guess the big guy got what he wanted, and he just moved on to another fish in his tank of gullible guppies.

After 3 weeks of silence and some major disappointment in myself for being a bad judge of character, I'd all but forgotten about Magnum when I got this text from him: *"Please stop messaging me. I had fun the other night, but I'm not interested in being tied down right now. Sorry if you felt that I led you to believe otherwise."* Clearly, Magnum forgot to delete my number and he had me confused with "ucompleteme14, 15, 16…" or however many others he'd moved on to and through, since our big night together. My reply, even as a linguist, was the best I could have ever conjured, under the circumstances; *"LOL."*

Meet You At The Bar

Lesson learned, I guess. Magnum was more of a mangy mouse than a mountainous gentleman, but who really cares? By showing his true colours (and early on), he enlightened me to the fact that online dating can be brutal, and you certainly can't judge a book by its cover.

Now, remembering that this online dating thing was supposed to be just for research purposes, I decided to try a little experiment to see just how awful men can really be. I enlisted the help of two (slightly) younger, very attractive women I knew. These ladies created profiles on "my" dating site and added their gorgeous photos. Instantly, they were inundated with a flood of messages from horny men. Together, we viewed and vetted their profiles, only picking "good guys," who were looking for long-term, serious relationships, and not just hookups.

The (game) plan went something like this: if a guy was interested in me (and I in him), we would wait and see if he matched and contacted either (or both) of the other ladies to try to "date" them, too. Time after time, after time, after time (Cyndi Lauper style), the guys who wanted to meet me, always wanted to meet one or both of my friends. Understanding that this was par for the course in the world of online dating, and people were free to date as many people as they wanted, I was cool with being one of many prospects. What I was not cool with, however, was getting bumped (and lied to) because someone "better" came along.

Each time I made specific plans to meet up with a guy, one of my friends would offer the exact same date and time to meet the same guy. Every single time, the guy cancelled on me. Something always came up, preventing Mr. Wrong from meeting me: *"I have a sick kid,"* or *"I have to work late,"* or whatever other lame excuse he could think up, was provided, while at the same time, he was solidifying plans with one of the other lovely ladies.

Over five days, the ladies and I managed to make dates with the same six guys - all complete horn dogs - each one bumping one or two of us (after making very solid plans) for another. We sent all six of these useless players to meet us at a specific bar, at a specific time, and all together. We told each one of them to sit at the bar and wait. When all 6 of them were there together, oblivious to our trap, and patiently waiting for their date to arrive, the three of us showed up together and sat at a table beside the bar.

One by one, each of the guys saw the three of us sitting together and figured out that they'd been set up, and they bolted. Not surprisingly, they were cowards, and not one of them had the guts to confront us. And for a change, these dudes got to feel what it was like to be played. We agreed that we all dodged some bullets, taught the bad boys a valuable lesson about respecting women, and best of all - we thoroughly enjoyed a useless men-free night together.

The "Rules" of Online Dating

Although the online dating thing was starting to feel more like reality than research, and my dating disasters were filling me with self-loathing and emptiness, I still decided to cast my line, one final time to see if there were any great, or at least "normal" catches out there.

To my relief, I found one very normal-seeming guy. His pictures and profile were nice. He was a tall, (sort of) handsome professional, just a few years older than me, and he had a couple of kids. He also passed the first test by having no LOLs in his dating profile. And, according to the chemistry test that the site conducted, we were a 96% match. Now how could I pass up a chance to pursue a date with someone who was only four percent better or worse than I? I was pleased to find that when I reached out to Eric, he and I seemed to hit it off immediately - well, at least within the confines of our new and strange texting relationship.

For a few days, we got to know one another through texts and phone calls, and slowly, our conversations became more casual, and I started to enjoy our fun and playful banter. Eric was intelligent and articulate, and he was able to poke fun at himself as much as I could. He made no inappropriate sexual advances, and I appreciated the slow pace at which he moved things along. I started to think that maybe the dating site, with its 96% compatibility score, got it right, and Eric may just be my almost perfect match yet. When he finally asked me out a week after we first started chatting, I was happy to accept his invitation. We made plans to meet for drinks at a cozy bar in my neighbourhood.

I arrived a bit later than he (to make my grand entrance, of course), and I was pleased to instantly recognize him from his pictures. I think he took a big sigh of relief, too, when he saw me, though his fidgeting told me that he was a little bit nervous. His anxiety instantly calmed my nerves because I felt that I had the upper hand. He was obviously more attracted to me than I was to him - bingo!

After a few sips of wine, I was relaxed enough to dig a bit deeper than our surface conversation about work and kids. And for research's sake, I decided to explore the psyche of an online dater. I asked him (casually, of course) several questions; "*So Eric, how long have you been on the dating site? How many dates have you had? Have your dates ever resulted in a relationship?*" And, on and on the "interview" went.

Talk about pulling someone out of his shell! These simple questions made this guy's eyes light up like a Christmas tree. He loved talking about his dating experiences and sharing his expertise on the matter. Over the next hour, Eric shared with me the "rules" of online dating. He implored me; "*Don't even think about giving out your last name until at least the third date,*" before scolding me; "*I find you to be far too much of an open book. Your texts are too long and detailed and you've revealed more about yourself than you should have. Don't you know how dangerous that is?*" The conversation proceeded this way for a while.

As he spoke about his actual dates (36, including me - and all of them, well-documented and probably given a rating out of 10), he continually referenced the online dating site as if it were some kind of playbook or even a religion. After my second drink, and not being able to get a word in edgewise, I was starting to feel like I was being put through a Scientology processing session.

Through Eric's very generous sharing of the rules, I learned that I disembodied all that online dating was supposed to represent. I was too friendly, apparently more attractive than my photos (which is a no-no for some reason), I shared too much information about my career, family, and friends, and I had the nerve to expect the same from my date. Near the end of the processing session, I was exhausted and relieved when the bill arrived. It signalled the end of our "meet," Apparently in the online dating world as I now know, the first get-together is not a real date, it's called a "meet up," or just "meet" for short.

While I was sitting on the fence, thinking that there may be a chance (in hell) that I'd see this guy again, he squashed that chance by fiddling with the bill so long that I finally just threw down my credit card and paid the damned thing. *"Anything to get the hell out of here,"* I thought. To make matters worse, Eric took the bar receipt that I had paid - to claim as an expense, no doubt. What a useless windbag. Talk about disappointment. If this was the best that online dating had to offer, I was resolved to meet the usual freaks I attracted, organically, or just remain single, like a sensible woman.

Alma's 50 Shades of Fuckin' Eh!

My sister Anne's friend, Alma is amazing. She's Spanish, sexy, bold, and fiery (to put it mildly). Alma has never suffered fools lightly, and she has no trouble asking for what she wants or telling it like it is. Since her own heated divorce, Alma loves being a single lady again, and she carefully picks who she spends her valuable free time with. Alma is also the most sex-positive woman I have ever met. She makes no apologies for her routine of hooking up with (much) younger and fit hotties, who have incredible stamina in the sack. I think every woman secretly wants to be like Alma.

One night I was at Anne's place for dinner, and Alma joined us. After a few salty margaritas, the conversation got a little raunchy, as Alma shared the juicy details of a recent night, where she claimed she had the best sex of her life. I, of course, was all ears.

"*I usually find Canadian boys dull, especially in bed,*" Alma started. Then, "*…they lack skill and passion, although I have to say, French-Canadian men are an entirely different breed.*" Alma prefaced this revelation, by sharing that she'd recently joined a dating site that catered to age-gapped relationships – more specifically, mature women and younger men. "*It's like being a kid in a candy store,*" Alma excitedly told me as she described the sea of profiles on the site, that feature tall, ripped, and gorgeous young men. I asked Alma if she'd mind having her story shared with my readers, and she was thrilled to expose her salacious dirt to help me out. Here's what she had to say:

"*Like I said, I felt like a kid in a candy store. The guys on the site are all hot, sexy, and perfect for plucking. Not that any of these babes have a desire for a long-term relationship, but that's okay, I'm happy to share some cougar love with these little cubs for a night or two.*

There was this one guy, Francois, who was perfection. He was 28, six foot three, he had olive skin and beautiful hazel eyes. And to top it all off, he was very funny and smart… pretty much the perfect package. And his French accent was 'tres adore-ab-la.' (It was funny to hear Alma with her Spanish accent, trying to sound French). *Even though we spoke on the phone, I was a bit concerned that Francois could have been a catfish. He just seemed too perfect.*

I've found out the hard way that dating sites these days, have so many bullshit profiles, with stolen pics of models, especially on cougar sites, where they're trying to extort cash from desperate older women. There was a little voice in the back of my head telling me that this guy was too good to be true, but I decided to keep going anyway. After talking for almost a week by text and phone, I agreed to meet Francois for a drink at the lobby bar in The Drake Hotel (on the west side of Toronto). When I walked in, the place was packed, and I started to relax a bit. I got there fifteen minutes early - just enough time to scout out the room for the best possible place to land and take a trip to the ladies' room to make sure that my hair and lipstick were perfect.

When I emerged from the ladies' room, I looked everywhere for my small screen God, but I didn't see him. So, I took a seat at the end of the bar and waited to see if (a) he would show at all, or (b) the balding, pudgy guy sitting two seats away, who couldn't stop staring at my legs, was going to lean over and introduce himself to me as "Francois." After fidgeting with my phone, applying another layer of lipstick, and downing a shot of tequila, I decided to get out of there. I figured that at least the place was busy enough that no one, except the chubby guy at the bar, would realize that I had been stood up. At that point, I was sure that Francois must have been a catfish, and maybe next time I'll learn to trust my instincts.

Just as I was heading for the exit, a long, buff arm grabbed me by the shoulder and gently swung me around. It was him, Francois, and was even more perfect in person. He kissed me softly on the lips and whispered, 'Hi gorgeous. Do you really think I'm going to let you escape that easily?' Without saying another word, he led me by the hand to a dark quiet booth in the corner of the room. I sat down and he pushed himself in, tightly beside me. He really was perfect. He had a glass of Tempranillo wine waiting for me. I told him in one of our many conversations that it was my favourite Spanish wine, and he obviously remembered. He picked up the glass and held it to my lips for me to take a sip. I quickly learned how hard it is to drink while holding your breath and pinching yourself in disbelief.

As he continued to crowd my space, he confessed that he'd gotten to the bar even earlier than I did and he watched me the whole time... applying my lipstick, fidgeting, downing that shot of tequila, and looking all around like a crazy lady. He also shared that it turned him on to see a woman so excited and nervous to meet him. I don't think I said two words. I just drank my glass of wine, while he paid the bill, and I eagerly followed him out the door like a puppy.

We took a cab to his place, not far from the bar. It was the main floor of a house with two bedrooms. It was kind of grungy, but I didn't expect much more from a man in his 20s. He had a roommate but apparently, he was out of town for work, so Francois assured me that we didn't have to worry about making too much noise. I felt so alive! Francois was a beautiful lover, and very giving in bed. Francois was very confident too, and I could tell that he'd had lots of experience with older women. I really didn't want the night to end, but I knew that this likely wasn't something that would last beyond the night."

Alma went on to tell me that as she had predicted, she never saw Francois again romantically after that night, although they did meet for a coffee a few days after their beautiful night together. She said he seemed very different than when they met up at the bar. The cool, sexy charm was gone, and he seemed kind of edgy, nervous, and dishevelled. Before she even sat down, Francois asked Alma, if she'd mind lending him a few thousand dollars, as he'd lost his job recently, and he had some urgent expenses to take care of, like covering his rent and needing to book a flight home to Quebec City, so that he could attend his mother's 60th birthday party.

As Alma was sharing this disappointing news, she chuckled, *"I knew it was too good to be true – he was just looking for a 'Sugar Mama.'*

I told him that if he wanted me to pay for sex, he should have just been upfront about it." She said that Francois didn't even look surprised when she accused him of this, so clearly this had been his routine with other unsuspecting older women.

When Alma and Francois left the coffee shop, they went straight to the nearest ATM, where Alma took out $200 and gave it to Francois, telling him, *"This is all you're getting. My years of experience are worth something too. Consider this severance. Have a beautiful life, kid."*

When Fishing Season Was Officially Over

Alma got me all fired up about the Cougar dating site, even though I was well aware of the risks. While I couldn't make myself join the seedy site, I sure enjoyed her stories, and decided to look for my own babe on POF.

The short-lived story goes like this. I met a handsome younger guy named Zack (doesn't that just say it all). We clicked, had a beautiful "relationship" for about 2 months (I only saw him when my kids were with their dads), and we "made love" a lot. Out of the blue, Zack dropped me like a hot potato - I think for an older (than me) woman. Clearly, old chicks were his "thing," and he'd decided that he'd shared enough of his "thing" with me, and he was gone just as fast as he came.

Useless man? Sure, but going back to what I was saying about expectations earlier, nothing could hold more true - you can't be disappointed when you have no expectations. During this little hunting and conquering phase of my life, I had zero expectations with Zack, and another hottie or two - each more physically spectacular than the previous, and each (so-called) relationship

184

ended in a fiery ball of lust. I finally realized these boys were good for my ego, but not for my mind or my heart. Their uselessness was useful in that they taught me about what I was really looking for, a break from boys and men for a while. And with that, I hung up my fishing pole and closed my online dating profile for good... That is, until I decided to go fishing one LAST time.

18

POSERS, BREADCRUMBERS, AND CATFISH – OH MY!

(Or…'Online Dating Part 2' – because Part 1 wasn't exhausting enough)

Since I first discovered the not-so-magical world of dating apps, online prospects have evolved or devolved, depending on what side of the device you're on. In the scary land of AI and "Deep Fakes," it's getting harder and harder to sniff out the real men, from the phonies. Even if you do connect with a real live boy, their "story" can be deceptive, disappointing, and even dangerous.

POSERS

The Fat Bank Account Trick

It's an old trick; a guy gives a girl he just met, his phone number, written on a bank slip, showing that he has oodles of cash in his bank account. This is a great aphrodisiac for gold-diggers, and a solid tactic for men who hope to have a chance with them.

I work for a big Canadian bank and recently went on a "field trip" with a colleague who used to work in the ATM division. While he was telling me all about these impressive machines and how they work, he shared a funny story about a trick that the young guys he used to work with would use, when they went out to nightclubs, hoping to get lucky with women who were out of their league. They had access to demo ATMs and would print out fake bank receipts, showing balances in excess of $100,000, to make it look like they had tons of money.

To unsuspecting prospects, these guys seemingly had mountains of cash in their accounts, according to the piles of fake bank account receipts in their pockets. Not surprisingly, these young men were a huge hit with the ladies. However, the cars they drove didn't measure up to their seemingly fat account balances, and the girls quickly got wise to their BS. At least the illusion was fun for them, while it lasted.

BREADCRUMBERS

Poetic Justice

Last year, my friend Maya and I went to New York for a weekend of great food, fabulous shows, and cool parties. Near the end of our first night on the town, we ran into some friends who were locals, and they took us to an exclusive (secret) bar with the type of people we like to meet. I couldn't tell you where the place was on a map, but I can tell you that the sophisticated lounge was packed with polished gentlemen, and fashionable ladies, and there was lots and lots of champagne flowing. We had a blast!

When I was ready to leave, Maya told me she wanted to stay for *"Just one more."* She was captivated by a seriously hunky (slightly) younger man, and they were deep in conversation about worldly and romantic stuff. "Randall" seemed amazing, and worthy of Maya's discriminating criteria for a potential mate. As promised, she managed to pull herself away, after *"Just one more,"* leaving Randall wanting much, much more of her. It was the perfect exit to a great evening for Maya.

When we got back to our hotel room that night, Maya filled me in on the juicy details of Randall's fascinating and jet-set world, and for the first time in a long time, she was excited to keep the conversation going. Before they parted ways, Maya shared her phone number, and the next morning she awoke to the most poetic, lovely text message from Randall:

> *"Maya, it was such a pleasure meeting you last night. I was lost in our riveting conversation and your beautiful eyes. It's not a line when I tell you, it felt like we were the only two people in that room. I can't wait to get to know you on a deeper level, and I'm excited to plan our next rendezvous. En attendant je penserai à toi." (Until then, I will be thinking of you).*

Their online communication began with full-steam-ahead fervour, and with a message like that, it felt like there would be no stopping this train to a town called, "True Romance." Although Maya didn't have time to meet up with Randall before we left the Big Apple, she did make loose plans with him to meet in the coming weeks – either in New York or in her hometown, Toronto.

As the weeks went on, Maya received similarly poetic texts from Randall, and she always replied promptly and thoughtfully. Each time, there was radio silence for a few days before Randall would reply. This seemed to be Randall's pattern. He'd wait a few days, send a sexy text, promptly receive one back from Maya, then nothing. I explained to Maya that Randall was a classic "Breadcrumber." That is, someone who *"makes plans with you but cancels or they don't show up, and they seem too busy for you...and they*

188

might even go absent for periods of time." But like any self-respecting woman, Maya decided that breadcrumbs were for the birds, and she had no interest in that type of "relationship."

The last time Randall sent Maya a text message, she left it on 'read' and him on ice for a few days before sending this one last response; *"If you were a loaf of bread, what kind of loaf would you be?"* to which he not so poetically responded, *"Huh?"* That's the way the Breadcrumbers crumble, I guess.

When in Rome

Amanda Chatel, a writer specializing in sexual health, mental health, and wellness, recently penned an article on Bustle, a digital magazine aimed at young women, about the phenomenon of breadcrumbing. At the time of writing the article, Chatel was herself involved in a breadcrumbing relationship, while she was in Rome, Italy. In her article, Chatel shares her personal experience and thoughts on the disturbing dating trend.

Straight From the Horse's Mouth

"Breadcrumbing is when someone wants to call it quits, but instead of disappearing into thin air or telling you they're not interested, they continue your texting relationship... it's worse than ghosting because it's more sadistic... Ghosting is a coward's instant way out of a relationship, whereas breadcrumbing is a slow and painful death of a relationship.'

How it Started

I'd only been in Rome a couple of days when I received a message via Facebook from an Italian guy who was inquiring about my job as a sex and relationships writer. I immediately got defensive, as he seemed to be

189

mansplaining me, so I attempted to shut him down. But he kept sending me messages and I told myself that the language barrier might be what was impairing my ability to read his tone correctly, so I let my guard down a bit and eased up.

After much badgering on his part, I decided to meet him. I had zero intention of dating anyone while I was here in Rome and was only on Tinder because I find the cultural differences from country to country to be really fascinating. But with this guy, I figured since he made such an effort to track me down, I could give him a few minutes of my time. And, if nothing else, it would make for an interesting story.

The "Dates"

I let him come over to my place on a Saturday afternoon because, despite what I interpreted as mansplaining and some fair share of aggression on his part in wanting to meet up with me, I live in a main square here in Rome. So, if anything went awry and I needed to yell out the window for assistance, there'd be hundreds of people to call out to.

He showed up with wine and we talked for hours and hours, with nothing physical happening. I learned that Italians don't have a word for 'dating'. He fancies himself an expert in relations between men and women, from a psychological standpoint, and he thoroughly enjoys hearing himself speak, among other things.

After hours of talking, we went to get food, which was followed by lots of sex well into Sunday, and then him making me dinner on Sunday night, before leaving. It may not have been a 'date,' according to him, but we did spend 30+ hours together and it was, surprisingly, really fun!

The second time I saw him, just a couple of days later, we got food and had lots of sex again. As one does. We also talked a lot about intimacy, connection, honesty, and communication. All the stuff that makes for a great relationship – romantic or otherwise. I found myself opening up to him in ways that usually take me forever to do. In the couple of days that had passed, he'd been texting me a lot; texts that were riddled with 'baby,' a term that I'm not a fan of, but one that I find European guys just love to use, so I deal with it. He was really cute and funny in those texts. He also sent me recordings of him singing, because he has a hell of a voice on him and a penchant for singing 'Dick in a Box' - No joke.

It was also on this 'date,' that I suggested we take the train to Napoli to get pizza that upcoming weekend, to which he responded, 'I never make plans in advance.' Well then. He left at 5 a.m. that morning.

Having only received a of couple texts from him in the couple of days that followed, I went out on a limb to see if he wanted to hang out on Saturday. He did. He came over with an expensive bottle of wine and proper wine glasses that he had just bought because this Airbnb flat doesn't have proper wine glasses. He also put a cute note on the box, which led me to believe he actually put thought and effort into this whole thing. It was quite adorable.

When we went to dinner that night, he went out of his way to find a place with lots of porcini mushroom dishes on the menu, because they're my favorite. There was a lot of handholding and cuddling going on — so much so that I was like, 'OMG, Chatel, he is really into you! You should totally move to Rome and be with him!' Actually, not so much of the latter, but it did cross my mind, because of the pizza.

Again, he spent the night, and we spent all day Sunday together, and he made me dinner before he left. That night I got a 'goodnight, baby,' message before he went to bed.

And So Began The Breadcrumbing

On Monday, I sent him the usual, 'I hope you're having a great day,' message and got nothing back. I assumed he was busy. When I finally heard from him several hours later, all I got was 'thanks.'

Later that night I texted him about an Italian song I heard on Master of None, followed by an inquiry about his plans for the following day. When I heard back, some 12 hours later, he ignored the part about the song and gave me a short reply about how he was tired. I mentioned something regarding his ambition, which he shot down with, 'I'm not ambitious.' Fine; don't be ambitious.

I didn't even bother to contact him the next day and he didn't bother to contact me either. But then I caved a day later and wished him a good day. His response? 'Thanks, you, too,' with improper grammar and no 'baby.'

Days went by and I heard nothing. So, I called him out on his behavior. His response? 'Baby, how are you? Baby, what makes you feel these things? I can't understand why you are in this negative state?' To which I told him to stop insulting us both. Then the texts turned cold, immediately dropping 'baby' from the equation again before I even had a chance to see him and tell him to his face that I knew what he was doing. It was at that point I was forced to look at myself in the mirror, facepalm, and admit what I didn't want to admit: He was breadcrumbing me.

Where I Am Now

At this point, I haven't heard from him at all in several days and I'll be damned if I reach out. I will not be breadcrumbed by some guy who thinks that such behavior is even slightly OK. Ghosting isn't OK, benching isn't OK, and breadcrumbing isn't OK.

Exactly when did we, as a society, become so rude? I have never, would I ever, treat someone with such flagrant disrespect even if I wasn't sure what I wanted from them or with them. I, unlike this guy and every other person who thinks this is an appropriate way to handle things, would suck it up and be honest. I mean, this guy claimed to be all about honesty and communication, and he can't muster the necessary integrity for two lousy seconds to put those two things into motion? Come the eff on, dude — you're 33; not 15.

I don't know if he's going to attempt to breadcrumb me again or if he'll just disappear. If he does try to, I don't know if I'll ignore him or tell him exactly what I think of him, colorfully decorated with a few dozen expletives. But what I do know is that breadcrumbing is sh*tty; it's no way to treat people and what he has done has reduced us both to stereotypes: He's the assh*le guy and I'm the woman sitting over here condemning all guys while wondering what I did wrong when, in fact, I did nothing wrong.

I'm not sure what will happen to him; if he'll ever find what he's looking for in the way of love and relationships, but I am sure that if he continues to treat people this way, he's going to have a very lonely life. However, that's his cross to bear. I leave Rome soon and will be on the beaches of Barcelona for the month of June. I guarantee, by July 1, I will have forgotten his name. In fact, I already have."

CATFISH

Just Do It!

With dating sites being packed with more fake profiles and bots, than real live men (and women) these days, nearly everyone who's been on one of these sites, has crossed streams with a catfish. It's certainly happened to me, but I don't really like to talk much about my horrific catfish experience, as it ended with the Police being called, and a restraining order being served. I think I have PTSD from the whole scary, scary situation, and I have definitely learned my lesson, the hard way.

The guy who catfished me was smooth. We "met" during the second long year of the COVID-19 pandemic, and I had my sick, elderly mother living with me at the time, so a contact-less "relationship" was the only possible option for me. I was grateful that "Jake" seemed fine with taking things slowly, and he certainly didn't rush me to meet up with him. In the weeks and months from when we first started chatting, we regularly exchanged pictures, we followed each other on Instagram, and we chatted on the phone, multiple times daily. Not only did Jake have a fantastic personality, but he was also a total hunk – he was 6'4, had a muscular build, and the most beautiful green eyes.

We were both working from home at the time so we could easily steal a few moments throughout our days to check in with each other. I was a Content Writer for a Transportation Tech Company, and Jake had the coolest job of anyone I had ever known – he was a Shoe Designer for Nike. He loved my sense of style, and he often shared his shoe designs in progress, and he asked my opinion about colours and other detailing. Jake was so thoughtful and romantic – he often sent me lunch and other treats through Uber Eats, and he regularly asked for updates about the well-being of my "roommates"– specifically my mom and my youngest daughter. Everything about Jake was perfect... but in retrospect, he was a little too perfect.

About 6 months into our "relationship," I pushed for Jake to meet with me, "live and in person." He lived alone in a gorgeous, spacious condo in Toronto (he had shared many pics), and we'd both had our COVID-19 vaccines by that point, so I felt it was a safe and the logical next step, to move things forward.

Like every predictable catfish story, the guy bailed on me. It happened time and time again, and it was always last minute... you know, once I'd made arrangements for my daughter to be cared for, and I was dressed (up) and ready to go. After the third or fourth cancellation, I reluctantly admitted to myself that Jake was definitely a catfish, and I asked him for a video chat. Of course, that didn't happen. Instead, he sent me a picture of a boarding pass, with his information on it. He was apparently heading to New York City for an emergency meeting at Nike's American Head Office. His boss had died suddenly from a heart attack, and he was needed in New York, straight away. Foolishly I almost fell for it, except in examining the ticket, I noticed that the departing and arriving airports had the same 3-letter airport code. In my head, I kept repeating the Nike tagline *"Just Do It... just bust the motherfucker!"* When I called him out on the bogus boarding pass, he naturally ghosted me. It was devastating, to say the least, but at least I'd gotten out of this disappointing situation with just a bruised ego and a bit of a broken heart.

For several weeks, I felt a lot of shame and anger about the whole situation. I couldn't figure out what the guy's deal was, and I was having a hard time trying to forget him. The whole thing just didn't make sense to me. He was thoughtful, kind, and generous (sending me food, flowers, etc.), and he most definitely didn't try to extort money from me. I was genuinely baffled. What was also baffling, were the sheer number of photos and videos that my catfish possessed of the infamous Jake, and the fact that my attempts at reverse-searching those photos produced no results.

A few weeks later, I was on Netflix, looking for something (anything) that I had not already watched during my marathon binge-watching sessions during the past year of the pandemic. I stumbled upon a new(ish) Bruce Willis action movie called *Hard Kill,* and I decided to check out the trailer. Lo and behold, my catfish boyfriend "Jake" was co-starring in the film. His character was aptly called "The Pardoner," and his real-life handle is Sergio Rizzuto. A quick search of Sergio, turned up several social media accounts, loaded with photos that "Jake" had sent me over the past 6 months. The revelation of Jake's true identity triggered me, and I decided to reach out to the number I'd been texting for so many months, to see if he'd respond, and if I could finally get some answers to my many questions.

To my complete shock, "Jake" had unblocked me, and was almost expecting my text. I told him that I knew the whole story, and his cover was blown. I asked him to do the right thing and come completely clean. What did he have to lose? He agreed to tell me about his motivation for Catfishing me, but only in person. My biggest mistake in this whole sorted mess was agreeing to meet him.

I met Ren (Jake's real name), at a park, so that we could go for a walk and talk. Ren was a short, young, pudgy Asian Canadian guy, who had a baby face. He confessed that he baited me, but only because he was lonely, and his attempts to meet someone online with his real pictures, were pointless. Like a fool, I took his bait once again and decided to get to know this seeming nice but sort of pathetic soul, to see if we could form a real friendship.

As I got to know the real Ren and started to trust him, we began spending more time together and formed what I thought was a true friendship. Spending time with him helped me comprehend his past actions (not that they were okay!), and it also helped me to find closure for the feelings I still had for the man I believed he had been for so many months.

One day when we were together, Ren took the liberty of hacking into my phone. Like a fool, I left my phone unattended for a few minutes, and he must have seen me punch in my very easy password at some point. With this, he was able to 'mirror' my device. I didn't even know what mirroring was until a "Genius" at my local Apple store, told me that this was what was happening to me. Screen mirroring technology allows a phone, tablet, or computer to wirelessly share an exact replica of its screen on another device.

This meant that Ren could see and hear my every move going forward. He received copies of my texts, he knew my exact location 24/7, and he had access to my emails and all my social media. In short (because there is so much more to this story, and not enough time or pages to get it all out), this guy was dangerous! He became a stalker, he turned violent, and I needed to involve the Police to make sure he stayed away from me, and my family.

Since the painful incident, I made a promise to myself that I would never attempt to meet someone online again, even if it meant I'd be single for the rest of my life. From the following stories I gathered from people willing to share theirs with me (and the rest of the world) on Reddit, it's evident that Catfish are common, difficult to detect, and they can cause endless damage to those who fall victim to them.

The Happy Ending

"I accidentally connected with someone on Twitter, and we started texting each other daily. Gradually, our conversations became longer and more frequent. He eventually confessed his feelings for me, and I made plans for us to meet in person. However, he kept making excuses and cancelling our plans. This went on for months. He then told me that he had been diagnosed with cancer and was undergoing treatment.

When I started asking questions, his answers seemed very strange. I felt that he was lying to me. I got angry and decided to drive to his town to confront him. When I arrived, he refused to meet me and confessed to me by text that 'he' was actually a woman, pretending to be a man. As I was leaving town, I drove past a gym that the man in the photos (she had sent me) supposedly worked at.

On a whim, I decided to go inside and see if I could find the guy in the pictures. I soon found myself talking to the real man behind the photos, and I explained to him that someone had pretended to be him online. He was shocked but happy to get a chance to meet me. Long story short, we arranged to meet up later that night, and we've been seeing each other ever since."

- thefoxrain

Double Duped

"In mid-August 2023, I messaged a man with a handsome profile picture through an LGBTQ dating site. He stated he lived in Kazakhstan and was 25 years old. He sent me several pictures and he was extremely attractive. We quickly delved into each other's lives. We primarily communicated via email, which in itself was suspicious. However, the emails quickly became passionate and intense. I shared much of my life story with him and my

background. I developed feelings for him after a few weeks. He was kind, caring and compassionate. He was empathetic, and intelligent and seemed to have a good life. However, our communication was still just via email. I chalked it up to time differences of 11 hours and he also told me he was a nurse in a hospital. However, I wanted to hear his voice and wanted to be closer to him.

Ironically, after 3 weeks, he initiated the request of wanting to talk on the phone via email. I graciously accepted and I was very excited to hear my new love's voice. 24 hours went by, and no call was received. I asked him if he could call me again but did not ask why he didn't call the day before. He finally called the next day. His voice was deep and handsome sounding. However, my intuition told me something was off. I couldn't explain it, I just had this odd feeling that his voice did not match with the pictures he'd sent me. The phone call was only 6 minutes long, and I could sense he felt rushed, like he wanted the call to end quickly. Again, I disregarded the 'off' feelings I had, and just went with it. I asked myself, if I wanted to pursue this man, I needed to learn to trust him. Trust is key in a relationship, especially long distance, right?

I received a 2nd call from him 1 week later. This time it was out of the blue. He did not give me a heads-up, and he just called me. I was very happy at the time because in my mind this meant he was making more effort towards our communication.

By this time, we were about a month in, and he had already expressed that he was in love with me and called me his 'soul mate.' This was very endearing, and I wanted to reciprocate by telling him the same thing. But something in me told me to wait and not say I loved him. I told him I was hesitant due to our distance and only speaking for 1 month - 95% of which *was via email. He said he understood and would be patient with me, once again demonstrating that kind, gentle and understanding nature I was so deeply attracted to.*

We began discussing meeting in person. He told me he had a 1-month vacation he could take from work anytime, and he wanted to use it to come see me. Oh, I was so thrilled. I thought finally I could meet this nearly perfect man of my dreams and spend time with him. It was like a fairy tale come to life.

We settled on meeting in November. He explained to me the cost of both tickets and a travel visa. He told me about the company he was contacting for the visa, the airport nearest him, airline details, etc. The intuitive voice in my mind was quickly deafened by the ever-growing voice of love and adoration for this wonderful man I thought I knew. He sent me a copy of his airline ticket itinerary with dates, flight numbers, etc. He even told me he borrowed money from his mom and sister to cover all the costs. He never once asked me for money or financial assistance.

However, my joy and excitement quickly changed when I found his pictures on someone else's profile on Instagram 5 days ago. My close friend asked me if I did a Google image search on his photos. I did with a few of them, but not all of them. At this point, I thought what the hell, why not? His last photos didn't appear anywhere, he was travelling to see me in 1 month, what could go wrong?

I quickly learned he used someone else's photos. I was absolutely devastated. I was also ashamed. I asked myself, how could I not know he was lying about his pictures?

I politely confronted him the next day. I told him about the profile and that it had the pictures he sent and asked him to explain himself. 24 hours went by with no response. After 48 hours or so, he responded. He admitted he catfished me. He admitted he was not confident in his own appearance, so he took someone else's photos. I was still clinging to some hope that this relationship was repairable, so I told him how hurt I was, and called him out on his manipulative behaviour. He stated he wanted to be more honest and upfront with me, so he sent me his 'real' pictures. I image-searched again, and 2 came up on a private Instagram account. No name, age, or location, just a username with no profile pic. Go figure huh?

It's now been a week since I discovered the truth, and man - this fucking hurts. I now realize I was manipulated and tricked. I also realize I ignored signs/red flags. My advice? ASK QUESTIONS! and listen to your intuition. That gut feeling that tells you something is wrong, listen to it. And you may find more often than not that you have this feeling for a reason."

– FruitySpook

19

GIRLS JUST WANNA HAVE FUN

"Cinderella never asked for a Prince. She asked for a night off, and a dress" – Keira Cass

Sometimes, we just need to get out of the house for a little female (only) bonding time. But is the cost too high? Wives, girlfriends, and especially moms can all relate to needing a night off - a night to hang out with the girls and forget your work troubles, the dishes, the diapers, the homework, the household, and the never-ending piles of laundry. But at what cost?

Yes, at what cost, indeed? Before I met my first husband, my mom had warned me: *"When looking for the man you want to be with for the rest of your life, make sure he's not the type who makes you earn your freedom."* I never really understood this advice until I was deep in the trenches myself - that is, married with kids. My husband's oh-so-important job meant that he worked a lot of long hours and travelled constantly. When he was home, he was tired, grumpy, and useless. I ended up doing everything - the cooking, cleaning, caring for the kids (and him), and this was on top of my very demanding 9-5 job. I was always dying for a break. Occasionally, when I managed to get out of the house for a couple of hours, things never went smoothly. The guilt he piled on me before I was able to escape for some much-needed time to myself was overwhelming, and my husband's disapproving groans and griping when I returned, would extinguish any joy I had experienced during my brief moment of freedom.

At least I'm not alone. I think most women can relate to this phenomenon. The multiple phone calls and texts we receive throughout our (rare) night "off," asking us when we'll be returning, are all a ploy to ruin our evening and get us back home soon (where we belong - ha). If we do manage to check our guilt at the door before we go out for the night, we'd better take advantage of our short window of freedom. My advice: Live it up, sisters, because we know that the second we walk through that door at the end of the night (think Cinderella at midnight when all returns her living hell), we are right back where we started. Only this time, the house is a disaster, and the kids are in bed with spaghetti sauce in their hair, and they most certainly did not have baths or brush their teeth. That my friends, is the price of personal freedom!

Being a single mom now, and getting every glorious second weekend off, this is an old issue for me. But the memories - ah the nightmares, more like it, have me thinking about this once again. Why is it that men think of themselves as babysitters and not fathers to their children? Every time I walked in the house after a girls' night out and got that look or "the guilt" rather, from my hubby, I kept wondering if I should be throwing my man a fifty-dollar bill, before driving him home to his parents' house.

Wake up boys - it's 50/50, remember? You scratch my back, and I'll massage yours for ten days straight after a girl's night out.

Pat's Penance

Pat is my mom, and she's earned her right to tell the gosh-d darned truth about the useless men in her life. Remember, my mom's unheeded advice about not being with a man who makes you earn

203

your freedom? Apparently, those words of wisdom were for others, not Pat. She learned the hard way, while married to my father, that she had to dig her way out of the trenches.

When I asked Mom to elaborate on her own experience, she told me that her husband would very firmly announce every Saturday and Sunday morning, *"I'm off to play golf."* There was no beating around the bush, there was no asking for permission, there was no having to work his way out of the house. He did what he wanted. Of course, my mom never felt she could announce that she was going to take time for herself. Even when she had to attend mandatory work events (she was the Director of a college fashion program), she would work up the courage to ask him if she could go out; *"James, I know it's a lot to ask, but do you think you could watch the kids on 'XX' date for about three hours in the evening? I don't want to inconvenience you, and I know the kids are a lot of work, but I really should go."* Of note, the "XX date" was always many weeks in advance.

My dad had plenty of notice and could therefore not use a work meeting or golf plans as a legitimate excuse. This didn't help any. It just prolonged my mom's agony. My dad would never just give her "permission." Rather, he'd torture her for the weeks and days leading up to her work event with questions like, *"When is your fashion thing again?"* and *"Are you sure your sister's not available to keep an eye on the kids that night?"*

Don't get me wrong, Pat was never outright denied the right to go out by my father, rather she was made to feel like it was his gift, and a huge sacrifice for him to occasionally watch his own children. It sounds old school, but heck, this still happens to women all the time. And these are women who vowed they'd never turn out like their mothers.

I once asked my mom how she justified this double standard and unfair behaviour in her own mind. She replied with a simple one-word reply: *"Brainwashing."* When asked to elaborate, she went on to tell me that my dad made it very clear from the start that *"Your job owns you from 9:00 a.m. to 5:00 p.m., Monday to Friday. Your family owns you from 5:00 p.m. onward, and every weekend."* He repeated it often enough, that she started to believe it. Simply, he brainwashed her. Although this stuff is a reality for plenty of women, it's still shocking to realize that many men feel that way about their wives. My mom said that she blames herself for this treatment because she helped to solidify the rules early in the game, with her compliance. She gave my dad permission to essentially act as the "leader" of the household - therefore, he made all the rules. Worst of all, she abided by them.

Now, at her ripe young age of 83, Pat proudly shared with me the turning point that led her to finally take her freedom back. Apparently, one time there was an all-women's event she wanted to attend, and she told my dad as much. When he asked her if she needed to go, she summoned up all her courage and said, *"No, it's not mandatory that I attend. However, I would like to go, and I could certainly use a night away from you and the kids. In fact, I plan to make a girl's night out a regular thing from now on, so deal with it, James."* After that, my mom simply announced that she had plans on "XX date" (without giving my dad much notice), and that was that. Surprisingly, my dad didn't say a word, not even when the kids gave the dog a really tragic haircut one night, while Pat was out at a fashion show.

Joyce's Jolly Jerk

Joyce lives an unhappy existence as the wife of a passive-aggressive man. In public and with her friends, Stan has always been the charming, funny, life of the party, walking into any room with a big warm smile on his face and, always addressing the women with *"Hello, my lovely ladies."* I have known Joyce and Stan for some time now. Our kids played soccer together, and we often had play dates at each other's homes. In observing their husband-and-wife dynamic, I always felt that Joyce was a bit unfair to (poor, sweet) Stan, because she didn't reciprocate his warmth; often rolling her eyes when he was pouring on the charm.

One day, when Joyce came for a visit with her kids, she seemed agitated. When I asked her what was wrong, she told me that she and Stan were not getting along. He'd been out with his friends after work every night for the past week, and she was exhausted and needed a break. I was surprised to hear this because Stan was always so attentive to Joyce and the kids, and he was very big on openly promoting the importance of family time. I told Joyce that she was in luck because my kids would be spending the night with dads 1 and 2, and that she should tell Stan that we were going out for drinks when he got home from work. This, of course, meant that he'd be responsible for watching his children for the night.

At first, Joyce got a little twinkle in her eye, obviously excited about the prospect of getting out for a little adult girl time. Then, her demeanour changed as she told me it just wasn't possible for her to go. Apparently, this wasn't enough notice for Stan, and he wouldn't be too pleased with her for going out without him. I told her that this was nonsense and that it was Friday! Without asking, I grabbed her phone and called Stan at work. I told him that his wife was tired of being cooped up at home and that she could use a little girl bonding time with yours truly. When I got off the phone, I told Joyce that it was all set. Stan was completely understanding and sweet about her getting out, and that she had nothing to worry about.

Joyce's grim demeanour didn't change (which seemed odd to me), but she still agreed to go out later that night. A few minutes after we arrived at the restaurant, Joyce went to the ladies' room, but left her cell phone on the table. When her phone started ringing, and I saw that it was Stan calling, so I answered. When I said *"Hello,"* the voice on the other side was not the Stan I'd ever known. In a teeth-gritting, grumbly, and intense voice, this is how he replied, *"Who the hell do you think you are, getting your idiot friend to call me up at my workplace and humiliate me like that? Your place is at home with the children, not out picking up men in some sleazy bar with your sad, single girlfriend. You'd better tell her you don't feel well and get your ass home now if you know what's good for you."* Then he hung up. I was still shocked and mortified when Joyce emerged from the washroom, and I suddenly understood why she never softened to Stan's warm and loving public persona. It had all been an act.

Rather than tell Joyce what had just transpired, and cause her additional stress, I told her that, unfortunately, my ex called and my youngest was sick, and she was asking for her Mama. I asked if she would mind if we left so I could drop her home and pick up my little "Goo." I assured Joyce that we'd plan another night soon and asked her for a rain check. Joyce looked relieved as she stood up to leave. Not so coincidentally, I never saw Stan again, and that rain check with Joyce never happened.

20

USELESS MEN IN POLITICS

"It is better to keep your mouth closed and let people think you are a fool than to open it and remove all doubt." - Mark Twain

It's almost an oxymoron: Useless men in politics! The list of men and their memorable incidents of ridiculousness are truly tireless. There's not much to consider or argue but, rather, let the facts speak for themselves. Remember this tiny sampling of political suicides by useless men:

Only In America

Dan Quayle: A minor yet international slip-up by former Vice President Dan Quayle, launched a frenzy and a long-running joke. Quayle led a spelling bee for sixth-grade students while visiting an elementary school in New Jersey in 1992. To his credit, he was working from an inaccurate flash card prepared by a teacher, when he corrected William Figueroa, 12, as he spelled "potato" on the blackboard, making the boy add an unnecessary "e" at the word's end. Quayle is (really) old now but he still has yet to hear the end of it. The media assault for this goof was truly relentless. The young Figueroa crystallized the effects of this incident on Quayle's public image when he said that it *showed that the rumours about the vice president are true… he's an idiot."*

Bill Clinton: On January 26, 1998, Bill Clinton famously denied his affair with Monica Lewinsky when he told the nation, *"I did not have*

sexual relations with that woman, Miss Lewinsky." However, Clinton later confessed that he did, indeed, have an *"improper physical relationship"* with Monica Lewinsky, a 24-year-old White House intern, at the time. For his deceit, Clinton became the second president in American history to be impeached by the House of Representatives, though the Senate later acquitted him.

John Edwards: The former United States Senator from North Carolina, and democratic party presidential candidate, admitted to having an affair in August 2008 with Rielle Hunter, a filmmaker hired to work for his presidential campaign. The illicit union even produced a child. The allegations, initially published in late 2007, were denied by both Edwards and Hunter. In fact, Andrew Young, a key staff member in the Edwards 2008 presidential campaign claimed paternity of Rielle Hunter's child (born on February 27, 2008), to shield Edwards from the scandal. The story gets even more messed up, considering Edwards' wife Elizabeth was diagnosed with incurable cancer. On January 21, 2010, Edwards issued a statement admitting that he was the father of the child in question. After the admission, Elizabeth Edwards announced that she was divorcing her husband.

Arnold Schwarzenegger: The former governor of California, actor, and once world-class bodybuilder, admitted to cheating on his wife Maria Shriver, who publicly defended him against allegations of sexually inappropriate conduct with women during his campaign trail. While he didn't specify how many affairs he'd had before Shriver filed for divorce in July 2011, Schwarzenegger admitted to an affair with *Red Sonja* co-star Brigitte Nielsen (while he and Shriver were dating, according to Schwarzenegger), as well as with another woman - his family's long-time housekeeper, Mildred Patricia Baena.

Nine months after Schwarzenegger and Baena had their affair, she gave birth to Schwarzenegger's son, less than a week after Christopher, his fourth child with Shriver, was born. This scandal ultimately led to Shriver's filing for divorce

Donald Trump... Enough said.

Canadians Aren't Much Better, Eh?

The major difference between an American and a Canadian politician is their height of public humiliation. Americans operate on a world stage, so their blunders are magnified, while Canadian political scandals tend to be chaste affairs that usually involve boring subject matter like railways and tainted tuna. In researching Canadian political scandals, the cases have been well-documented by province and timeline, though few would register with your average Canadian citizen today. However, there are still some, nine (so far), to be exact, that will go down in our Canadian history books as the most salacious misdeeds by useless Canadian elected officials:

John Edward Brownlee: Alberta's fifth premier was forced to resign after he was sued for seduction by Vivian MacMillan, an 18-year-old daughter of one of Brownlee's political allies. There was much speculation that Brownlee had been the victim of a political set-up after he noticed he had been followed on a country drive by one of the girl's teenaged suitors and a prominent Edmonton lawyer and Liberal party supporter. The case eventually went all the way to the Supreme Court, which sided with MacMillan.

The Munsinger Affair: Gerda Munsinger was a German prostitute and alleged KGB spy who seduced several cabinet ministers in the Diefenbaker government, of the late 1950s. Among them was the associate minister of national defense, Pierre Sevigny, who signed Munsinger's application for Canadian citizenship. The scandal was a well-kept secret among Ottawa politicians until 1966, when Liberal justice minister Lucien Cardin, fending off an opposition attack in the House of Commons on his handling of security breaches, asked *"What about Munsinger?"* By then, she had been deported, but reporters tracked her down in Munich, where she openly admitted to her numerous political affairs.

Margaret Trudeau and the Rolling Stones: Margaret Trudeau, wife of Prime Minster Pierre Elliot Trudeau, spent her sixth wedding anniversary without her husband, instead partying with the Rolling Stones at a Toronto nightclub, and later in Mick Jagger's limousine. The rendezvous sparked rumours that she was having an affair with the band's frontman. She later disappeared to New York. The scandal signalled the end of the couple's tumultuous marriage, but Margaret Trudeau denied having affairs with any members of the Rolling Stones, later telling a conference on mental health, *"I should have slept with every single one of them."*

Francis Fox: The 38-year-old solicitor general was the youngest member of Trudeau's cabinet and a rising star when he was forced to publicly admit that he had secretly arranged for a former mistress to have an abortion and had forged her husband's signature on hospital records granting her permission for the procedure. The relationship didn't last and neither did Fox's marriage. His political career, however, survived. Fox resigned as solicitor general but went on to be re-elected and reappointed to cabinet. He was made a senator in 2005.

Graham Harle: Alberta's solicitor general, was discovered by police parked outside a seedy Edmonton motel with a prostitute in his government car. The 51-year-old Harle claimed he was investigating the province's prostitution industry and had concluded that the trade didn't *"appear to be a problem right at the moment."* He stepped down from cabinet after the public refused to accept the story of his undercover operation.

Bob McClelland: The British Columbia industry minister and one-time Social Credit leadership contender Bob McClelland, admitted he had paid $130 to *Top Hat Escort Service* in 1985 to have a prostitute sent to his hotel after having *"a fair amount to drink."* His dalliance was uncovered after a police investigation into the escort agency uncovered his credit card details. McClelland resigned in August 1986 after testifying at a trial into Top Hat's activities.

The Wilson-Tyabji Affair: British Columbia liberal party leader Gordon Wilson, was fresh off a surprise victory that catapulted his party into official Opposition status when he appointed 27-year-old Judy Tyabji as his house leader. It didn't take long for rumours to start that the two, both married, shared more than just political leanings, though both Wilson and Tyabji vehemently denied any affair. Wilson resigned as party leader the next year just as Tyabji was dumped as house leader by the party. They later came clean about the affair, left their spouses, got married, and quit the Liberals to form the short-lived, Progressive Democratic Alliance.

Maxime Bernier: The star of Stephen Harper's Quebec caucus, was forced to resign as foreign affairs minister after admitting he had left classified government documents at the home of his then-girlfriend, Julie Couillard, a woman who had previously dated two Hell's

Angels associates. Shortly after they broke up, Couillard gave a tell-all television interview about the relationship, which she followed up with a book.

Justin Trudeau: Canada's current Prime Minister, and son of former Prime Minister, Pierre Elliot Trudeau, Justin Trudeau has had more than his fair share of scandal and controversy in the 7-plus years since he took office. Here's a quick run-down of Trudeau's top 5 scandals:

1) He broke conflict of interest rules by vacationing at the Aga Khan's private island, over Christmas on year.

2) He found himself a laughingstock after a trip to India, where he and his family enthusiastically dressed in various local costumes, to the bemusement of Indian officials.

3) He was dealt the hardest personal blow during his 2019 election campaign when a handful of photos came out of him dressed in blackface, a racist caricaturing of Black people.

4) SNC-Lavalin, a Liberal-connected firm in Quebec, faced charges regarding alleged bribes to officials in Libya.

5) Trudeau, and former finance minister Bill Morneau, had personal connections to WE, a charitable organization, when Trudeau shared that WE would run a student grant program, which was part of COVID-19 relief. The contract to WE was given via a sole-source agreement and was not an open competition

21

BAD INFLUENCES

"Men are afraid that women will laugh at them. Women are afraid that men will kill them." – Margaret Atwood

An article written by Angelina Jaya Siew, entitled *"Alpha-Male Influencers Are The Poster Boys Of Modern-Day Misogyny,"* speaks to the growing popularity of toxic social media influencers who embrace an "alpha-male lifestyle." Siew noticed that while *"casually scrolling through TikTok, I am bombarded with videos of brazen men and their bulging muscles, who often objectify women and preach about what an ideal male is supposed to be: dominant, psychically strong, and wealthy."*

Andrew Tate is the epitome of a toxic alpha-male influencer, as are the duo behind the FreshandFit podcast. There are many (many) other influencers who fit this bill, but why bother giving them any more airtime, and unworthy attention, than they've already sucked from us.

Andrew Tate

On December 27, 2022, self-proclaimed entrepreneur, professional misogynist, former kickboxer and (scary) online influencer, Andrew Tate, 36, sent a boastfully hostile tweet to climate activist Greta Thunberg, 19, about his large sports car collection. He wrote, *"Please provide your email address so I can send you a complete list of my car collection and their respective enormous emissions."* The lame loser was clearly hoping to provoke Thunberg, by mocking her commitment to climate change. Instead, she demolished him, and gained an unprecedented 3.5 million "likes" on Twitter with these 9 little words; *"yes, please do enlighten me. Email me at smalldickenergy@getalife.com."*

That ego-deflating exchange with Thunberg would be one of Andrew Tate's last, before being arrested, along with his brother, "whatshisname," on December 29, 2022, on charges of organized crime, human trafficking, and rape. Some women who came forward with details of Tate's crimes have publicly posted the disgusting and vile things he has said to them.

Just talking about this D-bag gives me the shivers. But sadly, Tate (or "Taint" as I like to refer to him), is dangerous for several reasons. Most notably, he directly threatens social equilibrium. Many young boys and men view Tate's radical and degrading views towards women, as enviable.

Tate's influence with a young male audience gained traction when he started getting views on social media like TikTok and Youtube, for saying outrageous things about women such as, *"If you put yourself in a position to be raped, you must bear some responsibility,"* and *"Why would you be with a woman who's not a virgin anyway? She is used goods. Second-hand."* And this is my favourite Tate quote, as it's one of his few that are gender-neutral: *"Reading books is for losers."* Tate's deliberately provoking nonsense would be totally laughable if the guy didn't have some 6.9 million followers on Twitter alone, and his alpha-male videos reportedly garnering a massive 11.4 billion views.

Savanta, a fast-growing data and market research company used "Youth Omnibus," a monthly tracker of 16-25-year-olds, to find out how young people, feel about Tate. One in three (32%) young men said they have a positive view of Tate, compared to just 9% of young women.

To many it's obvious, Tate is an insecure, toxic a$$hole, who says whatever outrageous thing he can think of, to gain attention, and popularity. The majority of Tate's fans are younger boys who are still growing and understanding the world around them. To these boys, Tate is some macho man who fights, lives in a mansion, owns shiny fast cars and *"gets women."*

His tactic of being straightforward and preying on weaker vulnerable men and boys is how he gains his following. However, like many successful but dangerous influencers, Tate, laces his hate speech with some constructive and factual things, that can also have a positive impact on young men. In this regard, Tate isn't worse than any other contentious egotist that men seem to gravitate towards, and his basic message for young men is positive, *"… Stand up, be important, and strong, and good-hearted and God fearing as possible, and … work hard to achieve those things."*

Basically, he tells boys to take accountability for themselves and to work hard to be successful. This part of his message is a good thing, but (of course) it comes with a price. For just $49.99 you too can enroll in Tate's "Hustlers University," with about 100,000 'students' internationally, and learn many ways to make money between business models and investment strategies. This is nothing but a classic pyramid scheme, and these "students", who are mainly boys, with some as young as 13, are being tricked into reposting Tate's videos on all social media platforms (as Tate has now been banned from all social media).

For now, I'm just happy that Tate is behind bars, where he belongs. And the only following of him I intend to do from now on is to monitor the status of his pending trial, and hope that they convict the loser, jail him, and throw away the key.

FreshandFit

We know that alpha male influencers are fostering insecurity in men who may feel that they sorely lack the qualities of their weak-minded social media heroes. To make up for their self-doubt, they try their best to emulate their toxic traits. As mentioned, a copious number of other alpha-male influencers exist, such as the duo FreshandFit, who amassed more than one million YouTube subscribers, despite being banned from TikTok.

In October 2020, Myron Gaines, and Walter Weekes, founded the FreshandFit podcast. The hosts' appealing personality and their purportedly smart content on dating relationships, and self-improvement, helped the podcast quickly gain a large audience. As the popularity of FreshandFit increased, so did the controversy about its programming. The hosts frequently got into intense arguments with their visitors, which some people found inspiring, while others found harmful. The channel was criticized for encouraging toxic masculinity and preserving misogyny.

This influencer pair flagrantly displayed their sexist views through their podcast, even having a day called "*Womanizer Wednesday*" on their channel. They also denounced values such as fidelity, stating that, *"monogamy goes against a man's natural state, (while) sexual fidelity is a woman's natural state."*

We must ask *"What can we do to control the dissemination of this negative portrayal of men?"* For one, these misogynistic idealists need to be banned from social media platforms, where they can unabashedly spew their sexist views, and gain dangerous control over the unformed (and uninformed) minds of young people. When FreshandFit's combative demeanor resulted in multiple high-profile confrontations, things really started to change for the duo. While controversy might have increased the channel's prominence, it also catalyzed its demise. Viewers quickly noticed a surge in conflict between the guests during the course of the podcast's three-year run, as well as between the hosts themselves.

The hosts were criticized for being both sexist and inconsistent. Gaines and Weekes were frequently seen arguing with young men about the wisdom of devoting time and effort to "new-age females," and Gaines confidently claimed that treating modern women the same way as old-fashioned guys does not get the desired results. In an unearthed video that has now gone viral, host Gains compared women to vehicles and questioned why he should have to *"pay full price for a used one."* Fans rightfully found his comments repulsive and denigrating to women.

There was a silver lining in all this though, when Gaines revealed that the channel had been "kicked off the YouTube partner program." Oh well... Bye, bye FreshandFit! The controversial podcast's success and failure offer a sobering lesson in the advantages and disadvantages of creating internet content. Even though controversy may at first grab people's attention, it has a two-pronged effect that might ultimately do irreversible damage. Like many others, the FreshandFit podcast's hosts had to learn their lesson the hard way.

As a society, it's crucial that we acknowledge the true horrors of this type of content, with misogynists as the creators. This is not only a problem for young men who are fed unrealistic and toxic ideas, but also for women who are constantly subjected to cruel and vile comments, and threatening behaviour. The emergence of these negative influencers and their rise to fame is alarming, and we must teach our children to question who they are promoting, and why we are promoting them.

22

EQUALITY AND THE USELESS MAN

"Chivalry never died. The gentleman in most men did."
– S.L. Morgan

This gender equality thing is literally killing me, and many other women like me. Long gone are the days when a man would give up his seat on a bus or train for a woman, even a gut-busting pregnant one. I remember taking a streetcar to work when I was pregnant with my first child. It was only a 20-minute ride to my office, but some mornings I felt like a bowling ball would fall out of me and roll down the aisle if I didn't take a seat.

I clearly remember the morning that I mustered some courage, and approached a guy who was about my age (in other words, young and able), and asked him if he'd mind letting me take his seat. To my complete shock, he told me *"No,"* and shared that he'd been out late the night before and was too tired and hungover to stand. And if that wasn't bad enough, the two young, also able-bodied fellas sitting beside the hungover jerk, didn't come to my rescue either. At that moment, I wished for my water to break and cleanse the sins and the leather brogues of these classless men.

Over the years, I've started to notice a certain discomforting reality when it comes to men (not) being chivalrous. With every unopened door, stolen parking spot, and unlifted heavy parcel, I realized that I was truly on my own. Even my own husband (Number 1) decided I was physically incapable of needing help. When we moved into our first home, I alone, stripped all of the 70s psychedelic, glittery wallpaper from nearly every room of the house. I also painstakingly scraped the popcorn ceiling throughout, hung each pendant light fixture in four bedrooms and the dining room, painted most of the rooms, and I demolished a creepy backyard fence, before tackling the front and back gardens. My husband would have loved to help, I'm sure, but he was a busy guy who needed to spend all of his free time labelling and organizing his new wine cellar.

When baby number two was baking in the oven, it took my friend Maggie to point out that I shouldn't be lugging 30-pound bags of potting soil from my car's trunk to the back garden. Witnessing this one afternoon, she stormed over to me, grabbed the bag of soil, and in her best girly toss, threw the bag of dirt at Teffy, who was reading the paper and lying in a chaise lounge by the pool. When the black clingy soil burst out of the bag and into the pool, Teffy stood and screamed, *"What the hell is your problem, you crazy bitch?"* Maggie yelled back, *"I'm crazy? I'm crazy? It's your beaten-down little woman who's crazy enough to put up with your crap. She's carrying your kid for Christ's sake. Get off your fat ass and help her out. What is wrong with you?"* Barely acknowledging her, Teffy brushed the dirt from his flip-flops and defiantly sat back down to finish reading his paper.

At that moment, Maggie grabbed my hand, dragged me to her car, and drove away to her house. Although I was panicking about not being home when my two-year-old would wake up from her nap, I was assured by Maggie that Teffy would just have to handle things without me. Maggie worked on me for hours, trying to get me to see the light, and I reluctantly gave in, and stayed the night. I didn't call Teffy, or answer any of his (many) texts.

When I returned home the next morning, my hubby launched into me about abandoning him, and he went into great detail about how thoughtless my actions were, how selfish I was, and how he was burdened with having to make his own dinner. Not once did he mention our daughter. As usual, it was all about him, his inability to man up, and his perpetual disappointment with me. At that point, I was proud of myself for finally taking a moment for me (even if I needed to be kidnapped by my BFF to do it). Maggie had somehow gotten in my head, and that was a great thing. Teffy's rant suddenly started to sound an awful lot like Charlie Brown's teacher; *"Wah wah wah wah wah."*

At that time, I had just taken maternity leave from my job, and I wasn't due for another three weeks. I decided to take a break from my life with Teffy for a while, so I packed my stuff, my little girl, and my bulging tummy into my car, and took a drive to my mom's house, 2 hours west. We were moving in for a while. My so-called man would learn the hard way that he needed to step up to the plate, or I wouldn't be crossing the threshold of his Shangri-La ever again. Sadly, he enjoyed his "time off," and as you know, I eventually left Teffy, not long after my son was born.

Misogyny Hates Company

Although Teffy held the title of self-absorbed a$$hole for a long while, husband Number 2, could sure hold his own in that realm. At least Hubby Number 1 took me for a nice dinner once in a while to compensate for his complete and total uselessness in the kitchen, and he was always appreciative of the nice meals I made.

As for Number 2 (that label suits him perfectly), not only did he not cook, but he made a practice of taking his breakfast in the dining room, while the kids and I ate together in the kitchen. This guy was so self-absorbed that he didn't want to be interrupted while he read his morning paper. He seriously thought he was doing us a favour because it was his right to be grumpy in the morning, and if we brought out his inner Dr. David Banner (aka The Incredible Hulk) by interrupting his alone time, then our pancakes and Cheerios were upset by a visit from the green monster. He did allow me to do his dishes, though, before I got myself and the kids out the door for the day.

Ah, but all that toil must have had a silver lining, right? The odd romantic night out would remind us of the love we shared, and why we were married. NOPE! When I think back to our big nights out without kids and remember the seedy and cheap Polish pub, he used to drag me to, the words "odd" and "romantic" seemed to be interchangeable for Derek. When I couldn't stomach the thought of another night of pierogies and draft beer, I'd insist on going to a proper adult restaurant with linen napkins and a wine menu. These were always great nights for us. I got to dress up and feel pretty, and he got a free meal. I can't help but think of the famous Seinfeld episode where Jerry got to spontaneously fly first class and he ordered *"More of everything!"* Derek always ordered more of everything when I was paying - surf and turf, a $200 bottle of wine, after-dinner drinks, and dessert. On these nights, Derek loved having *"More of everything!"*

If I allow myself to think about it, it was truly humiliating that he had no problem telling waiters that his *"Old lady's picking up the tab."* I remember early on in our relationship, we used to frequent this quaint little Greek restaurant for lunch. After our third lunch together (and with the same man serving us), the waiter took me aside as I was leaving and said, *"Listen, this is none of my business, but I'm a Greek man. Greek men don't let their women pay, never mind repeatedly paying when they're on a date. This guy is a loser. Every time I bring the check, he heads to the washroom, knowing you'll pick up the tab, by the time he gets back. You really should reconsider this guy - you can do a lot better!"* Man, oh man, was that man right on the money. I should have given that guy my number. And he was cute too!

Even now, several years after our divorce, Derek's lack of chivalry still amazes me. Take this morning, for example. Toronto had one of the worst snowstorms ever. As he was dropping my daughter off at my home, he complained that I hadn't shovelled the walkway. I told him that I shovelled a few hours prior but that the snow must have accumulated again. I told him that the shovel was at the foot of the stairs and asked him if he'd mind clearing the snow on the (whopping) three steps, so that the kids and I wouldn't wipe out when we left the house. With a chuckle, he said, *"That's your job now honey."*

Sherry's Chivalrous-less Chumps

My friend's daughter, Sherry, shared with me that she's been noticing an unflattering trend with the men she has dated recently - they are outrageously cheap, and not chivalrous at all. Talk about a turn-off. Sherry told me that she'd rather be single than continue to suffer by having to spend more of her valuable time and hard-earned money on jokers like these. Here are some tales from Sherry's recent dates:

Mr. Cheap And Charmless

"I went out with this guy three times. On absolutely none of the dates has he paid for anything. Each time, when the bill came, he just sat there until it got awkward, and I'd say, 'halfsies?' Only then, would he reluctantly agree to pay his half of the bill. I felt like he was waiting for me to offer to pay it all. After our second date, which was just like the first, I suggested we stop for an after-dinner drink and dessert at a beautiful and romantic piano bar. He hemmed and hawed until I said, "My treat," then he excitedly agreed to take me up on the offer.

When we were seated, he asked the waitress for the wine list (which was odd considering that this guy had only drunk draft beer at our dinners), then he ordered a $30 glass of ice wine, and the most expensive dessert on the menu. To say the mood was extinguished, was an understatement, but he was still eager for a third date.

About a week later, I unenthusiastically accepted his invitation to dinner at his place. I wasn't really "feeling it" anymore but I felt like the least he could do was make me a meal or order me one! Like a proper guest, I brought a nice bottle of wine, which he opened and guzzled most of, before our meal. There were no appetizers to be seen, and nothing was cooking on the stove, but I was relieved when he excused himself to 'go and get dinner.' He lived in an apartment, so I naturally presumed that he was going to meet a food delivery person at the door in his lobby. About 5 minutes later, he returned with a pie-shaped dish, covered in tin foil. His elderly neighbour had given him her leftover chicken pot pie (from frozen), in exchange for feeding her cat while she was out. While I was recovering from shock, he removed the tinfoil, scooped the pie into bowls (not even plates) and microwaved them, before passing me my bowl of undercooked chicken pie.

He didn't offer me anything to drink, not even the wine I had brought, so I asked for a glass of water, which he poured from the tap. The mood was definitely killed at that point, and I just wanted to get the hell out of there, and home to my Netflix and chill (out).

When I said, 'Well, I'd better get going,' about 20 minutes after the disgusting 'dinner,' he didn't try to stop me. Instead, he just poured the rest of the wine I'd brought, into his glass and asked, 'Do you remember how to get to the train?' It was a 15-minute walk to the train station from his apartment, and the least the drunken jerk could have done was walk me there, but NOPE, that didn't happen. Strangely, about a minute after I left, he texted me, saying what a great time he had had, and he couldn't wait for our next date. Obviously, that never happened either."

Mr. Chivalry For A Select Few

"I went on a date with a guy who my colleague Lara introduced me to. She assured me that he was fun, good-looking, and had a great job. He sounded like a great man.

The plan for the date was that Nate would pick me up, then we would go for breakfast before he would drop me off at work around 10 a.m. This seemed like the perfect way to start the day, and it was a relatively low-stress, low-time commitment first date.

It was a winter morning when he drove up to the front of my condo. My friend was right. Nate was gorgeous. His smile could melt the cold away. He handed me a hot coffee, winked at me, and said: 'I was sneaky and asked Lara how you take your coffee so I could impress you.' Here it is. I hope you're impressed!' I laughed and told him that I was indeed impressed. 'This is going to be awesome!' - I screamed in my head.

We arrived at the breakfast place early, and they were just opening. Nate played the perfect gentleman as he opened and closed the passenger side door for me. As we were walking into the restaurant, there was an elderly woman who was sweeping outside of the restaurant doorway, clearing away the snow for patrons. To my surprise, my date dropped his empty coffee cup, right in front of the woman who was sweeping. He didn't drop the cup by mistake, he dropped it so that she could sweep it up and take care of his trash. I was completely taken aback, and I asked him why he did that. He said that because she was already sweeping, she could just 'take care of it too.'

I didn't say anything, but I saw the humiliation in woman's eyes, and that was enough for me. I bent down, picked up his empty coffee cup, and placed it in the trash can outside the restaurant. Nate didn't even acknowledge that gesture (which I made for the other woman). I then excused myself to the ladies' room and called an Uber. When I left the washroom, I walked past my date, who was by then seated, without saying a word. I got in the Uber, and I never looked back."

23

EMBARRASSMENT IS WORSE THAN USELESSNESS

"Women cannot complain about men anymore until they start getting better taste in them." - Bill Maher

I recently had lunch with my colleague, Liz, to catch up after the craziness surrounding the Christmas holidays. We both have kids, and like me, Liz hosts her entire family every year. My place is affectionately known as "Chez Ellie" to most of my friends, who think I'm crazy to host major holiday festivities, year after year. But I'm a traditional girl and my home is where my kids, my siblings, my extended family, and my band of misfit single friends, want to be over the holidays.

The kids always have fun, and the adults enjoy sharing funny stories over drunken afternoons, that last well into the evening. In sharing silly pics of the merriment with my pal, I asked her to reciprocate. She nearly started to cry as she told me, *"I can't find one decent, photo from the past week."* Liz went on to tell me that every single 'happy family' photo op had been ruined by her husband, Jarrod.

Jarrod's Holiday "Uniform"

"I don't have one decent picture of my family, because of Jarrod's uniform," Liz told me." *The asshole insisted on wearing his boxers, a stained KISS t-shirt, and nothing else for the entire week. And never mind the man boobs and the gut - the fact that he refused to shave or wash his hair for his 'week off' literally drove me to drink."*

As I poured the wine, I said, *"Drink up, sister, you deserve it."* I remembered those horrible days in my not-too-distant past with Number 2. He'd refuse to put on anything other than his tattered, yellowed football jersey and track pants, especially when I really needed him to be presentable (for me). And, to make matters worse, while the extended family ate Christmas dinner in the dining room, he chose to eat alone in the kitchen. That was his thing. I always hoped for Santa to come down the chimney and take him back to the land of the misfit boys.

A few months later (late February to be exact), I dropped by Liz's condo with Goo to have tea and some snuggles with "Chichi," Liz's sweet little preschooler. As we were having a proper girls' tea party, I noticed a big evergreen tree sitting solo on the third-story balcony. *"Strange,"* I thought in my ADHD mind, but I kept on dunking my digestives into my chamomile tea and forgot about it. A while later, Goo said to Liz's daughter Francesca (Chichi), *"Chichi, why do you have a Christmas tree outside?"* Chichi just laughed, grabbed Goo's hand, and headed for the playroom. I took one more look and said, *"Yeah, Liz, why do you have a Christmas tree outside?"* Embarrassed she said, *"Well Ellie, remember Jarrod's Christmas boxers and greasy hair? Why do you think I still have a Christmas tree out there? Jarrod's so fucking lazy and embarrassing, he can't be bothered to take the damn thing down to the refuse room. So now we're stuck. Christmas has been over for two months, and it's too late to dump the damn thing. It's gonna' continue to rot there—stuck in the cigarette ice pot - until spring, when it's warm enough, and I get up the nerve to take it down the elevator and throw the damn thing out, myself."*

I was killing myself laughing at that story, of course, as it was just one of many. Jarrod is one of those truly useless but loveable

229

guys. He drives his wife nuts with his antics, but the rest of the world gets a big kick out of him.

Here's a typical Jarrod story: Last New Year's Eve, I attended a party at their place. Everyone looked great - even the kids were wearing fancy clothes. And to Liz's elation, Jarrod was dressed appropriately, and he seemed to be on his best behaviour. The condo was beautifully decorated, and the party was a catered, elegant affair. There were about twenty-five to thirty people in attendance, and Liz's kids were adorably playing host and hostess to the guests, offering to take their coats and hang them up.

About halfway through the evening, after having a few too many scotches, Jarrod assembled everyone around their baby grand piano and said that he wanted to share his latest and greatest achievement. Excited to see what trick Jarrod had up his sleeve, most were surprised when he called his sweet four-year-old daughter into the room. As Chichi walked towards the piano, everyone was thrilled that Jarrod's "stunt" was really going to be the unveiling of a child-prodigy pianist. As Chichi got to the piano, she jumped up on the piano bench and cued her dad to start the music. Suddenly, a burlesque tune started to blare. The four-year-old proceeded to do a sexy striptease dance (without taking off her party dress, thank God), twisting her little body to the music, and rubbing her hips and tummy, as she blew kisses to the people in the room.

When the song ended, you could hear a pin drop. It was only when Chichi climbed down from the bench, grabbed a basket, and walked around the room soliciting monetary donations, that any noise could be heard. I think they were gasps, but it was hard to tell over Jarrod's roaring laughter.

Another Jarrod Classic

One day I was having lunch with Liz in the food court of our office building, and as usual, she was telling me ridiculous stories about her husband's antics. The latest involved dropping a forgotten lunch bag off to their daughter in her kindergarten class. Apparently, he couldn't just drop off her lunch, he had to drop by his 9-year-old son's classroom and embarrass the poor little guy by singing a crass little tune about farting. That poor kid! I asked Liz if Jarrod had always been this way. Without skipping a beat, she shared this little nugget:

"It was the first time he ever met my extended family. We were going to my cousin's wedding at a super swanky hotel. Jarrod was wearing an older suit that was hanging in his closet for at least a year. When he put it on, it was much tighter, because he'd been working out for the past year, and he'd gotten really buff. I remarked that the suit looked a bit tight around his calves, but he didn't care. He liked that he was finally fit, and he wanted to show off his toned legs. At the reception, we started talking to one of my cousins about investments or something, and I was really proud of how well-behaved and sophisticated Jarrod was acting. Things couldn't have been going smoother until Jarrod, who was my fiancé at the time, dropped his wallet on the floor.

When he squatted down to pick it up, there was the loudest ripping sound you have ever heard. People actually stopped their conversations and turned to look at what had happened. Jarrod had ripped his suit pants so spectacularly that the tear somehow stretched from his crotch all the way down to the bottom of his calf. In true Jarrod fashion, he had chosen that day to wear a pair of boxers that I had given him as a gag gift the previous Christmas. They had a picture of a dump truck on the butt, with the quote, 'Got Junk in the Trunk?'

There was just no coming back from that. He had to do his best to preserve whatever shred of dignity (and pants) he had left, so he quickly left the massive room, passing just about everyone and giving them a good look at him, and his shredded pants, as he walked. He did manage to grab and guzzle a drink from the bar, on his way out though. To this day, whenever my family sees Jarrod, they greet him with, 'Hey - Got Junk?'

24

GREAT UNCLES

"To get to a woman's heart, a man must first use his own."
- Mike Dobbertin

My mom spends her winters solo in Mexico now while my dad and his wife, Katie, spend theirs in Arizona. Arizona is dry, clean, and white. Mexico, by contrast, is steaming hot and gritty, with many artists' colonies. All the pieces have seemingly fallen into place for my divided parents. They are now, with their "own kind," happy in their differing ideas of post-retirement bliss. My mom is a painter and a damned good one at that. My dad's a golfer, and each round he plays is full of "gimmees." It's always been about winning versus the joy of the experience.

While my mom is away - taking a break from the cold, and the perpetual drama that surrounds her four adult kids, and her many grandkids, I do tend to get a bit lonely for the one who understands me, who I can call and cry to, and who can give me the best advice for every situation. While my mom is away and I'm virtually alone, raising my three kids and dealing with the rest of the family drama as it comes my way, I have two saviours. They come in the form of uncles. One is my dad's younger brother, and the other is my mom's. By some miracle, these two men who are now in their late 60s, managed to meet each other during their teenage years, and they've remained friends all this time.

My uncles, Terry, and Hal couldn't be more different from one another - just like Abbot and Costello, Mutt and Jeff, and the

Jolly Green Giant and his Little Green Sprout. But, like those famous duos, they somehow 'just work.' And to my great fortune, they are the most important older men in my life. I love them both dearly and will until the day I die.

While my Mama's away, the uncles come to play. We drink great wine and eat great food, that they've learned to cook since their wives left them, because they were useless. It's strange, but as an adult, well into my womanly years, I've come to appreciate these male relationships like no other. They are not my dad by a long shot, thank God, and they are not at all like my ex-husbands (again thanks to the mighty one), but they are older, wiser, and infinitely important to me. They are also a ridiculous source of material. I don't know if we reach a certain age when dirty old man humour just becomes 'humour,' but here are some typical, seriously corny, and crass uncle jokes from my most recent fun weekend with Uncle Terry and Uncle Hal:

Uncle Terry:

- What's the difference between a circus act and a chorus line? . . . A circus act has a cunning array of stunts.

- What do a computer and a blond have in common?... We don't appreciate either until they go down on you.

- I'll take 'The Rapist' for 200 Alex. . . .That's therapist, Mr. White!

- Is that a turtle skirt you're wearing, Ms. Pearl? . . No, why do you ask? . . . It looks awfully close to the snapper.

- What's the difference between a woman in a bathtub and a woman in church?. . . A woman in church has a soul full of hope.

Uncle Hal:

- Save your breath, Terry! You have to blow up your date, for later tonight.

- Should I call you for breakfast or just nudge you?

- Wanna' come upstairs and see the inside of my shower curtain?

- I'm so broke, I can't pay attention.

- Are you European? . . . Why? . . . You've got Roman hands and Russian fingers.

- What do rednecks do on Halloween? . . . Pump kin

- I'd rather fart and bear the shame, than never fart and bear the pain.

- You know, I once got a Viagra pill stuck in throat? I had a stiff neck for a month.

Next weekend, my Uncle Hal is hosting a family reunion. All the uncles, aunts, and cousins from my mom's side will be in attendance. After the reunion, and likely a few too many glasses of good wine, my uncle Terry is picking up my brother and I, and we're going to his place for an after-party and sleepover. I'm not sure which event I'm more excited to attend. Hal's party will be a great catch-up with the extended family, but Terry's afterparty will include rocking out to cool 70s tunes and gathering more material for my roster of funny family tales, and sick jokes.

Adventures With Uncle Jay

My brother Jay is a kind, generous, sweet, and funny person, but he can be a bit of a useless twit at times. Last week, he sent me a picture of himself while he was in the middle of painting the spare bathroom in his condo. For some reason, he thought black was a great colour for the walls and ceiling. As expected, he ended up getting more paint on himself than on the walls.

I must preface any stories I tell about Jay, by sharing that he is the type of person who perpetually has bad luck. He's always 30 seconds too late to catch his commuter train to work. He's the guy who didn't get the 'change of venue' memo for the high school reunion, and he's definitely the guy who gets a parking ticket while he's quickly dropping off lunch for his daughter at her school. Jay can be very lazy, and a bit entitled too. Although my children love him, they have some crazy stories about the things he pulled while he was babysitting them many years ago. These stories have only recently surfaced as he'd sworn my kids to secrecy. But now that they are adults who enjoy drinking, and getting a little loose-lipped, they love sharing old Uncle Jay stories, at family get-togethers.

Send In The Clowns

Jay used to love watching my kids at my place. When he got divorced (several years ago), his bachelor pad at the time was stark, to say the least. My place, on the other hand, was filled with all the creature comforts a single man could ever want; food in the fridge, a big comfy couch, a big screen TV, and all the streaming channels a boy (or girl) could ever want.

One night, I had a work event, and I asked Jay if he'd mind staying at my place to keep an eye on my son and daughter. He said, *"No problem, I'll get them some dinner and make sure they're bathed before bed."* The kids loved (and still do) their fun Uncle Jay, and I knew they'd have a great night together. When I returned home later that evening, I found the kids hovering over my brother, who was passed out on the couch. I asked them what the heck was going on. It was really late, and they had school in the morning. When they turned to face me, my jaw dropped. Their faces, hands, and pajamas were covered in Halloween makeup that they had dug up, and they were in the process of painting Uncle Jay's face like the clown from their favourite show, "The Big Comfy Couch."

KFC Anyone?

Another time that Jay was watching the kids for the night, he somehow managed to lose his wallet on the commuter train, on the way to my place. When I picked him up at the station, with the kids in tow, he neglected to tell me about his latest case of bad luck, for fear of being teased.

The kids were excited to see him, and he promised them a fun night that would include video games, movies, popcorn and their absolute favourite treat, Kentucky Fried Chicken. Before I dropped them off at my place, I tried to give Jay some money to pay for the evening's fun. As always, Jay refused the money and said, *"Don't insult me sis, you know how much I love to spoil my niece and nephew."*

When I got home a few hours later, there was the usual carnage – popcorn everywhere, piles of KFC chicken bones on plates in the sink, and I found both kids and Jay asleep (in their daytime clothing), in my bed, with the TV blaring. I felt that it had been a good night, all things considered. There were no injuries or broken furniture, and the kids were sleeping. Success!

Recently, at a family holiday dinner, my grown son Hank said to my brother, *"Hey Uncle Jay, are you ever going to pay me the $50 you owe me for the KFC? With interest rates, I figure you're up to about $185 now, but I'll let it slide."* It turns out that because Jay had lost his wallet on the train that fateful day (many years ago), and he was determined not to lose face with me, or break his promise to my kids, he simply "borrowed" money from Hank's piggy bank to cover the cost of the KFC. He wasn't counting on Hank having a memory like an elephant though, and he justifiably got the teasing of his life that night.

Again, Jay promised to pay back the money soon, but you know, *"No one carries cash anymore Hank,"* said Jay. After dinner, Hank found a solution to Jay's cash problem, by driving his uncle to the nearest ATM. Hank was happy to accept $100 for his trouble, and as a payout to end Jay's teasing.

Never Gonna Give, Never Gonna Give …

My daughter recently got into an elite science program, at a top Canadian University. She's one smart kid and has exceptional grades, but the program had very few spots, and the competition was fierce. We were all so very proud of her. Her Uncle Jay was no exception.

I held a celebratory dinner for Jules, and as always, Uncle Jay was in attendance. Before the night was out, Jay handed Jules an envelope, with $200 cash inside, and a very sweet and thoughtful note. As always, there was a little hidden message in his kind words for Jules:

"My dear sweet niece, Jules,

Never forget how far you've come, and I know you're

Gonna do great! As you move toward this next stage,

Give yourself plenty of room to make mistakes.

You only live once and you got this!

Up and up is the only way you'll go from here.

Never look back. We all know you're

Gonna be a superstar in your science program.

Let your strengths shine.

You deserve the world. One question...

Down to party with your old uncle still?

Love uncle Jay xxx

P.S. Read the first word of each line ☺

P.P.S. Sorry about the Christmas Card, it's all I could find."

25

THE BOYS IN MY HOOD (AKA "PETER PANDAS")

"I heard my name associated with the Peter Pan Syndrome more than once. But really, what's so wrong with Peter Pan? Peter Pan flies. He is a metaphor for dreams and faith." – Mark Burnett

There are very few women who are not familiar with the "Peter Pan Syndrome." This affliction is reserved for men who still behave like boys, and secretly vow to never grow up. As a suburban mom (with two ex-hubbies), in the shopping mall wasteland where I continue to live for the kids, I know this species all too well. These are long-time married, restless guys, who still play in organized hockey leagues during our long Canadian winters (and they not-so-secretly think they're the "Great One"). In the summer, they keep themselves "hot" by playing in baseball or soccer leagues, after their 9-5 work days. They also drink at local watering holes after each 'career-changing' game.

The 'Pandas' (as my fellow suburban moms and I call them) look like regular dads. They have beer guts, receding hairlines, and they make bad apparel choices - yet for some reason, after each game and a few pints, they somehow reclaim their studly single man personas, and they convince themselves that they are God's gift to women. As for the much younger, scantily clad barmaids who bring the Pandas pitcher after pitcher of premium beer, and plates of hot wings and nachos, they know how to pour, and "pour it on" thick. They forcefully giggle off the Pandas' inappropriate advances and accept that the odd unsolicited butt or booby elbow brush, is the price they must pay to earn the elaborate tips they get each post-game Tuesday and Wednesday night. You see, these bankers, lawyers, and accountants by day and 'Pandas' by mid-weeknight, have dough that the younger and more skilled sports "players" don't, and their tips are the size of their inflated egos.

There's a ridiculous but accurate portrayal of these charmers in the Farrelly brother's movie, *Hall Pass*. This story is about "Rick and Fred," two typical suburban husbands who are finding marriage difficult, so their generous wives give them each a "hall pass" to do whatever they want with whomever they want, for one full week. In one of the movie's best scenes, Rick and Fred, and a few other guys, end up at Applebee's, a popular (and cheesy) American restaurant chain that is packed with families. When one of the guys sarcastically asks, *"Is Applebee's really the best place to meet hot horny women?"* Rick (Owen Wilson) replies, *"Really? What are you thinking? Olive Garden?"*

This suburban man scenario isn't only for the movies, though. I occasionally visit these places with my single girlfriends past 9:00 p.m. when the masses of hungry families leave for their weeknight bedtime curfew, and we get the opportunity to watch these "boys" in action. It's hilarious, especially because I know most of these local guys, and they are still married to the women who used to talk to me before I became the neighbourhood divorcee and was therefore, ousted from the lonely but married hearts club band of wives. These guys are literally like peacocks - sucking in their guts, puffing out their chests, and posturing for every twenty and thirty-something "girl" who is forced to squeeze by them.

As for my fellow divorcees or never-married gals, nary a glace comes our way from these old boys, and really, who cares? We have the sixty to seventy-year-old men on our tails, and the entertainment value of their collective shenanigans is well worth the $9 suburban glasses of Sauvignon Blanc versus the $25 glasses of Sancerre with the "kids" in the packed lounges near downtown's financial district.

These days, I'm starting to feel like a broken record with my *"Thank God that's not my life anymore"* discourse that I bestow upon my giggling girlfriends, each time we visit these places. I too remember the days when my cad of a sports-loving ex-hubby (#2), would cross the finish line of our home base after a big game, and a night at the pub with the boys. He was always more than a bit drunk and always horny, waiting to share his testosterone-filled, amorousness on me. But that's just one more useless man memory that I'd like to forget.

26

PICKING MY BATTLES

" I don't always hate my neighbours – but when I do, it's just when they are at home" – The Most Interesting Man in the World (aka The Dos Equis Man)

It's unfortunate, but based on my personal experience, I've come to realize that some men can be ruthless, arrogant, and even bullies. As I've shared, I've certainly encountered and dealt with these types of men, both in my personal and professional life. However, what's most surprising is the audacity of some male strangers. Whether it's men on the street or men across the street, I have (recently) learned to stand up for myself, walk with my head held high, and protect my right to have peace in my own home, on the street, and everywhere else in my life.

Side-Walking - The Social Experiment

A few months ago, I decided to cut (way) back on drinking alcohol. I have long suffered from atrial fibrillation (Afib), an irregular heart rhythm that begins in your heart's upper chambers, with symptoms that include fatigue, heart palpitations, trouble breathing and dizziness. Drinking alcohol exacerbates the problem, so deciding to limit myself seemed like the smart thing to do. I have tried many times before, unsuccessfully. But like all women, I'm a work in progress, and I need to be gentle with myself.

To ensure my success in deviating from my wine-loving life path, I started reading voraciously, and I have learned a lot about the physical, as well as the cognitive benefits of living life, sans alcohol. Amazingly, and as promised by almost every author on the topic of sobriety, my brain fog has lifted, I suddenly have more energy and best of all, I'm sleeping like a baby for the first time since I was one. Another residual benefit has been improved self-confidence.

There's one particular book that has helped me with the not-drinking thing, and it's also helped me with making great strides toward greater self-awareness. That book is Holly Whitaker's, *Quit Like a Woman: The Radical Choice to Not Drink in a Culture Obsessed with Alcohol*. This brutally transparent feminist critique of alcohol and recovery cultures gave me several "*ah ha*" moments while reading. Whitaker openly attacks Big Alcohol (and Big Tobacco), for their calculated targeting of women in their advertising, and she connects the promotion of heavy drinking with systems of oppression.

As it turns out, low self-esteem appears to be a major symptom of heavy imbibing for many women. It makes us lose our inhibitions and often, our good sense of judgement. The aftermath is always the same – shame and regret. We do things we would never do sober, including putting up with bullsh#t and abuse from useless men. In one chapter, Whitaker talks about how women need to stop giving in to male intimidation. She shares that we need to "*learn to claim our right to take up space, to say our words, and to claim our desires.*" This even includes our right to own our side of the sidewalk.

Whitaker observed that women almost always move for men, most noticeably when passing them on a sidewalk. She claimed that she tried a little experiment where she refused to move from her side of the walk, and men were forced to literally stay in their lane. She was often body-checked, after their attempts to stare her down, and over, failed. While that observation was shocking to me, I realized (consciously or subconsciously) that I move for men ALL THE TIME – when I'm walking down the street, when I'm walking down the aisle at the grocery store, and even at work, when I'm searching for a chair in a packed boardroom, with limited seating.

Over the last few weeks, I have consciously stopped side-stepping for men and started side-walking. So far, I've been called a f*&%ing bitch, I've been scolded twice for tripping over large dogs, (whose long and unrestricted leashes afford them more right to the sidewalk than me), and I am currently icing a bruised arm from having to forcefully push my way through a drunk and disorderly male foursome, who were blocking the walkway to my home's front door.

I'll take the bruises any day. I now loudly and proudly say, *"Move over fellas."* The useless sidewalk stealers will just have to learn the hard way, that I will no longer be leaving my comfort zone or my place on the sidewalk, for them.

Karen and Her Husband

Okay, I call 'em as I see 'em, and there's a not-so-soft spot in my heart for the "Karens" of this world. The same goes for their husbands, though there's no universal label that does them justice, just yet.

These days, the term "Karen" rarely needs explanation but here's what I found on Wikipedia: *"Karen is a pejorative term used as slang, typically for a middle-class white woman who is perceived as entitled or demanding beyond the scope of what is normal. The term is often portrayed in memes depicting middle-class white women who use their white and class privilege to demand their own way".*

I have a not-so-neighbourly, "Karen" who lives across the street. I'm not sure what her real name is because she hasn't introduced herself, and she's been shooting me dirty looks ever since she and her husband moved in last year. This Karen lives with her equally entitled, and downright bullying husband, Mark. That is his real name, and I only know that because he told me so when he pounded on my door the other day.

For a little background: I live in a very affluent, mostly white, almost adult-only community near Lake Ontario. Lucky me, right? Well – sort of. I'm the ONLY renter within a 5-block radius in my not-so-pleasant-ville neighbourhood. I lost my ability for home ownership when my second ex-husband won half of the proceeds of the house I bought on my own, because it was the "marital home," and according to Ontario law, that was his right. At least he spent the dough on something good though – a 2-bedroom lakeview penthouse, that he now rents out for an inflated buck, while he's shacked up with his girlfriend and her 3 kids.

The other half of the proceeds of the sale of my home went to pay for my eldest daughter's 2-year residential stint at her rehab school (to the tune of $30,000 plus, per month). This was money well spent, mind you. But now I am a renter and will be for the foreseeable future.

As luck would have it, I found a lovely little turn-of-the-century historic home in a highly sought-after neighbourhood. The price was just right because the out-of-town homeowner wanted a reliable, long-term renter (Moi), more than they needed to cash in on the exorbitant price that their (extra) house would fetch, in the crazy-inflated housing market where I now live. This home is also close to fantastic schools, and it is a very safe neighbourhood. This is and always has been, a priority to me, as a single mother.

The neighbours surrounding my little slice of seemingly peaceful heaven, are self-important bullies who literally harass me constantly, about everything! They scold me for the state of my not-quite-perfectly-manicured lawn and garden, although I keep the property in tip-top shape, all by myself. Unfortunately, I don't have a team of dedicated, year-round groundskeepers to do the work for me, like they all do, and I feel like telling them, *"Sorry to disappoint you folks, but my only paying job gets in the way of my ability to maintain a perennially perfect property."*

My next-door neighbour is a treat too. He repeatedly knocks on my door, asking me for the name of my landlady (who lives in China), because he is determined to buy the property, only to knock down the house, and expand his already exclusive and massive lakefront estate. This, of course, would displace me and my youngest daughter – but he could care less.

Most recently, the neighbours have started squatting in my driveway – parking their cars here, whenever they feel like it, because there is no available street parking. Their own driveways are blocked by construction vehicles because their homes are under constant renovations. Don't you know, they need a spot for their luxury cars when they come to visit their homes? They don't care if they block my car in, or out, while they're occupying my driveway, and they certainly don't care about the constant noise pollution and never-ending dust and grime, that their perpetual home improvements are inflicting on my ability to live a quiet, peaceful, and dust-free life in my home, with my child.

Just the other day, "Karen" from across the street, parked her convertible Mercedes in my driveway while I was out getting groceries. She made sure to park with the tail end of her car at the entrance of my drive. This meant that I could not enter until she decided to leave. She parked that way to ensure that she could back out, unobstructed, of course. That was the last straw. I had had enough. I placed a not-so-nice note on her windshield telling her to *"Move your f*#%king car, and don't park in my driveway again, or I'll call the Karen Police, and have you towed. This is your final warning! Have a nice day ☺"*

Well, let me tell you… Hell hath no fury like the husband of a Karen scorned. About an hour after I got home and was in the middle of a Zoom video meeting with work, Mark marched right over to my house and started pounding on the front door with all his might. My daughter (whose bedroom is closest to the front door), was terrified. I had to excuse myself from my meeting, to answer the door and make the pounding stop.

It's safe to say that I put nothing past these a**holes, and I had anticipated and was prepared for the wrath of the Karens. When I opened the door, Mark launched into me with, *"How dare you leave such a vulgar note on my wife's car. You weren't even home, and you rent this place so it's not really your driveway. We have every right to park here if we want. Give me the name and phone number of your landlord…yadda, yadda, yadda."*

I stopped listening to the loser the second I opened the door, and he stopped shouting the moment he looked down to see the words on the T-shirt I was (purposely) wearing; *"NOT TODAY KAREN!"* I let the words sink in before Mark attempted to speak again, then I shut the door in his face.

Since that day, I've lined up my recycling bins at the foot of my driveway as a blockade. Another sh*tty neighbour just didn't get the hint though, and he decided to run the bins over, and park in my driveway in protest, and of course, in solidarity with poor Mark and Karen. I had that jackass towed – ha!

I've thought about moving many times in the last year because of my mortifyingly nasty and entitled neighbours, but Halloween is around the corner, and there are a few places I may just need to decorate with eggs and toilet paper first. Needless to say, Halloween by default, is 'Karen-hunting' season, and it's also my favourite time of year!

27

FRIENDS' IN "HIGH" PLACES

"I love my FedEx guy, cause he's a drug dealer, and he doesn't even know it … and he's always on time." - Mitch Hedberg

Okay, so I'm acquainted with 3 interesting moms, some of whose kids happen to attend the same schools as mine. They are each married to, ahem, regular family guys. The women all have upstanding, legitimate careers and their hubbies all have "J.O.B.s" too. One man is a freelance lighting technician in the film industry, another is a construction worker (on workman's disability compensation now), and the other is a banker type, in mid-level management. While these guys each have proper jobs, they are also classified as "urban entrepreneurs." According to the urban dictionary, an urban entrepreneur is *"someone who is a street hustler; someone who makes money selling illegal merchandise (or legal merchandise illegally) on the street or in an urban/ghetto area out of his residence or an illegal place of business (ex. warehouse, back of a grocery store, etc.)"* An example of this type of entrepreneur is *"one who: deals drugs, sells stolen electronics off the back of a truck, sells bootleg DVDs, selling items to people stuck in traffic, etc."*

The 3 sweet little families are much like any other in suburbia. The moms volunteer at their kids' school charity events, both parents sit on the sidelines of their kid's soccer and hockey games each weekend, and they all have a strong community presence. The only difference is that these families live rather lavish lifestyles for their income brackets, and they have incredible, almost palatial homes, expensive cars, and lots of extra money for trips to the Caribbean. *"How the heck do they have some much money?"* many of the jealous Stepford wives and their competitive hubbies, who live in the 'hood,' ask. Well, that's easy. It's because Daddy is a coke "dilla" (or "dealer" to you common folk), and they have piles and piles of cash to spend on whatever their little fast-beating heart's desire.

For the sake of this chapter, I'll refer to these couples as Sid n' Nancy, Kurt and Courtney, and Bonnie and Clyde.

Sid n' Nancy

I adore "Nancy." She's feisty and confident – all five feet one inch of her. She has gorgeous, long black hair (she loves extensions), big brown eyes, and a body that would make Helen of Troy jealous. Nancy is also one of the sweetest, and most generous people you could ever meet. Her hubby "Sid" is, well, not so sweet. He's a buff and gruff commercial construction manager, whose currently on disability leave, with a bad back. Because of Sid's situation, he is at home a lot. However, he seems to keep busy, entertaining a myriad of sketchy visitors who drop by their home each day, and at all hours - 9 a.m., 10 a.m., 7 p.m., 10 p.m., 11 p.m., 1 a.m., 4 a.m., and you get the point.

Sid's clueless neighbours must certainly think he's the most hospitable guy of all time. He never seems to turn away any of his short-term visitors, who enter the house through the side door of the 3-car garage. And Nancy doesn't seem to mind the constant traffic in and out of their home, even though she needs to get up early for her shift at the hospital, where she works as an Oncology nurse.

Although Sid is mostly home bound these days, he does manage to take off for a few days each month to meet with his side hustle business associates, whatever that entails. The details of those meetings are never disclosed to Nancy for *"for her protection."* When her husband was away one day, Nancy agreed to sit down with me and give me the real scoop on her life with Sid. The origin of Sid's successful side gig had already been revealed to me, when Nancy let the cat out of the bag, while she was "half in the bag" at a mutual friend's New Year's Eve party.

Nancy inadvertently shared with me that Sid is a drug dealer – cocaine specifically. However, *"Don't worry, he never sells to underage kids, and his clients are mainly the rich assholes from the neighbourhood."* When I approached Nancy in the parking lot of my youngest daughter's school and asked her to share her and Sid's story, she said she would as long as I promised to not use their real names. I agreed, and we made plans to have coffee at Nancy's place the following week.

When I asked her how she deals with Sid's dealing, Nancy avoided eye contact with me as she told me *"It comes with the territory,"* while serving me the most wonderful, freshly brewed Columbian coffee, and cocadas – delicious little coconut Columbian sweets. Sid and Nancy are both from Columbia, although Nancy moved to Canada when she was 13. They were introduced when Nancy was 18, through their mutual family friends, when Sid was sponsored by his uncle to move to Canada. They quickly fell in love and got married. Nancy went to nursing school and Sid, took a job with his uncle's construction company, and he helped with other unmentionable assignments after hours.

Nancy has grown to accept the fact that her husband is a legitimate, albeit injured, construction worker, and (more than) a part-time cocaine dealer. When I press her to talk about her fears as a dealer's wife, she continues, *"What can I say? I love nice stuff, and our kids and their futures are well looked after. I guess it's worth the risk."*

Occasionally, Nancy's mom takes the kids for a weekend. She lives a few hours east, and knows how hard her daughter and hubby work, so it's a labour of love to care for her energetic grandchildren for a few days. On these occasions, Sid, and Nancy love to throw lavish parties for their friends who are those "in the know." Like something out of the movie *Scarface*, all the women are attractive, plastic, and dressed to the nines, and the men are carbon copies of one another - dark, hairy, handsome, and dressed in their slightly shiny suits. While these events are always catered with elaborate spreads, the food rarely gets eaten because the copious bowls of party favours are also appetite suppressants.

One of the rare times I was invited to attend a Sid n' Nancy party, I played dumb and asked Sid if he was doing okay, given that he was on leave from his construction job. Sid's a smart cookie, and he saw my inquiry as an opportunity to justify his drug-dealing ways; *"Well since my back is F'd up and I can't support my family on my bullshit comp checks, what do 'they' expect me to do, sit around and be useless?"* I almost answered *"Eh badda boom, badda bing,"* But I kept my big mouth shut. I'm the type of neighbour that Sid n' Nancy like, and I intend to keep it that way!

Kurt and Courtney

Among the three women in the neighbourhood with husbands who have colourful careers, I am closest to "Courtney." She is a former Playboy Centerfold with waist-long blond hair (that she wears in a high ponytail most days), plumped-up lips, fantastic faux double D's, and a closet full of clothes that could rival J-Lo's. Courtney runs her own successful business - a mobile spray tanning salon, where she spends her days bronzing juiced-up bodybuilders, competitive cheerleading squads, and exotic dancers. She seems to do quite well for herself. Courtney has two small kids, a boy, and a girl, and she is extremely involved with their schools and extracurricular activities, between her mobile tanning appointments.

Courtney's husband "Kurt," leaves the house every morning (except Sundays) at 6 a.m. to "run chores," and he's back home between 7 p.m. and 8 p.m. nightly. Kurt's "chores" entail managing multiple indoor (illegal) cannabis grow ops, and they keep him busy year-round.

About once a month, Kurt joins the filmmaking world, where he works as a part-time lighting technician, for Film and Television production companies. Kurt loves being part of a film crew but that job, *"just doesn't pay well enough,"* Courtney tells me. With her hands on her well-toned hips, she shares, *"I'm a high-maintenance girl, obviously, and I need a man who can buy me what I deserve. I don't want some useless dude who toils away at a low-paying job and never has two dimes to rub together. And as know, I work hard to make my own money too, but you know me... I really like my bags, my shoes, and my five-star vacays, and I need to be comfortable. I feel absolutely no guilt about how we make our money, and anyone who has an issue with our lifestyle can go suck it."* Yep, that's my friend Court in a nutshell. She tells it like it is, but then again, so do I. I guess that's the tie that binds us.

Kurt, by contrast, is very low-key, cute, and cuddly, and by all appearances, he's a regular suburban dad and husband. He's the last guy you'd think would be running a $30 million-a-year weed operation. I guess it's why neither the government nor the cops have ever come sniffing around. In Kurt and Courtney's neighbourhood, Kurt plays the not-so-hard-working average Joe, with a hot, hard-working wife. All the neighbours scratch their heads, wondering how dopey-seeming, squishy Kurt, landed an ambitious babe like Courtney. The couple is content with the occasional curious remarks from their nosy neighbours, as long as their children are happy and well-adjusted, and Courtney gets to live the lux life she deserves.

Bonnie and Clyde

"Bonnie" is the friend of a friend. She's sweet, mild-mannered and for all intents and purposes, she's a regular suburban wife and mom. I've gotten to know Bonnie through my very close friend Kim, who attended private school with her in St. Catherine's, Ontario when they were teens. They reunited when Bonnie and Clyde moved to Mississauga, the town next to mine. The couple welcomed their first child about six months ago, and Bonnie's over the moon, and taking to her mommy duties like second nature. When she's not caring for her son Gus, Bonnie teaches Grade 2, part-time at a local private boys' school, and she can't wait until her son is old enough to start learning all that she has to teach him.

Of note, Bonnie has never tried drugs, and she pretends that they don't exist in her world. Clyde, by contrast, is a career criminal who did a fair bit of time in "the joint" before he moved to Canada from Detroit, Michigan and somehow landed a contract gig as an IT project leader, with a reputable financial institution. His slate in this country has somehow (mysteriously) been wiped clean. "*It's all about who ya' know,*" Clyde pompously told me when I asked him how he managed to pass the extensive criminal and background checks that ensue before you are hired by a financial institution in Canada. Clyde is a nice-looking, sharp-dressed man who knows how to pour on the charm. He makes me uncomfortable, but that may just be because I know what his nighttime job is – selling cocaine and other illegal substances to well-established clientele in the nightclub industry.

Aside from the fact that they're the only interracial couple in their extremely conservative, mostly white, old-moneyed neighborhood, nothing would draw attention to Bonnie and Clyde. That is, except for maybe the fifteen exterior cameras that are strategically placed around their beautiful property, and the bulletproof glass that outfits Clyde's white Cadillac Escalade.

28

MEN WHO ARE "JUST FRIENDS"

"If a woman has a male best friend, he's usually just her backup plan" – Author Unknown

It's often assumed that non-romantic friendships between men and women are unlikely, but our everyday experiences suggest otherwise. In fact, it's common for men and women to coexist as housemates, to work together, or simply hang out and grab a beer together, without spontaneously needing to have sex. I'd like to think that I'm a shining example of success when it comes to platonic male-female relationships, as I have several long-term (platonic) male friends.

However, research conducted by the University of Wisconsin-Eau Claire, USA and published in the Journal of Social and Personal Relationships, suggests that we may not be capable of being "just friends" with members of the opposite sex. The study revealed that the possibility of romance is often lurking around the corner, waiting to pounce at the most inopportune moment, despite our belief that we can maintain a platonic relationship.

I tabled this topic the other day with my brother Jay, while he was eating one of my home-cooked meals (of course), at my kitchen table. I asked him about the many friends that he had while we were growing up, who happened to be girls. He confessed that while he did have several female friends, he either slept with them or he wanted to sleep with them. I was taken aback (a bit) until I realized that his partner now, is one of his best friends from high school. They just so happened to rekindle their "friendship" on

Facebook when both of their marriages fell apart. He told me, *"You're dreaming in technicolour if you think your guy friends don't want to have sex with you. Remember Ryan Reynolds' character in 'Just Friends'? I promise you, every single straight guy, with a female friend, wants to f@ck her. Sorry to burst your bubble. That's just how it is. Why don't you just ask your guys friends if I'm right?"*

So, I decided to ask my guy friends point blank, *"Do you now, or have you ever, wanted to sleep with me?"* Here's what they had to say:

Ken, a former co-worker, and close friend for 9 years:

"Ha-ha – yup, busted! I wanted to sleep with you, from the moment we started hanging out at that work summer picnic, on Toronto Island. I got over it pretty quickly though, once I met your baby boyfriend, and knew that I wouldn't be able to satisfy your cougar needs. I'm happy that we're friends though. And you do give me great advice about women."

Gerald, a childhood friend of over 40 years:

"Yes, of course, I wanted to sleep with you. I still do (laughing). As kids, didn't you see how methodical and patient I was - becoming great friends with your little brothers, just waiting for my chance to get close to you? Well, we've been friends for more than 30 years now darlin' – and that's an awfully long time to be waiting to make my move. The truth is, we hang out, have some laughs, and enjoy a good solid time together. I genuinely adore and cherish our friendship, but I accepted a long time ago that we won't ever be knocking boots… that is of course, unless you want to?

"Shels," a housemate of a former boyfriend, and friend for 25 years:

"Is that a proposition? I'll happily scratch your itch if you scratch mine. Woof,oof!"

29

THE PERFECT MAN...

All work and no play makes Jack a dull boy. All work and no play makes Jack a dull boy...

I suppose I could have just written *"Lorem Ipsum, Lorem Ipsum, Lorem Ipsum, etc.",* which is the placeholder text used in design, before adding "real" content to a page. It helps writers and visual designers plan out where the final, polished content will sit, without needing to wait for the actual words to be written.

I also happen to be a huge fan of the Stanley Kubrick movie, *The Shining,* based on Stephen King's novel, and I thought that the content from Jack's book worked perfectly well here too. If you're not familiar with the movie, here's what you need to know... 'Jack Torrance' (Jack Nicholson) becomes the winter caretaker at the isolated Overlook Hotel in Colorado, hoping to cure his writer's block. He settles in, along with his wife, 'Wendy' (Shelley Duvall), and their son, 'Danny' (Danny Lloyd). Danny is plagued by psychic premonitions (Danny "Shines"). As Jack's writing goes nowhere and Danny's visions become more disturbing, Jack discovers the hotel's very dark secrets and he begins to unravel into a homicidal maniac, hell-bent on terrorizing his family.

My favourite scene in the movie is when Jack's wife discovers that he has spent the last months procrastinating, and his book is comprised of the same 'filler' content, "*All work and no play makes Jack a dull boy, All work and no play makes Jack a dull boy...*" written over and over again, on hundreds of pages, with his typewriter.

I guess what I'm trying to not-so-eloquently say, is that I have yet to find the perfect man, or even a really good one. Until then, I'll be waiting to add "real" content about him, to the page.

30

WOMEN ARE FAR FROM USELESS

"This is a man's world, but it wouldn't mean nothing
without a woman" – James Brown

There are many variations of the old saying, *"It's a man's world."* However, in my endless search for its origin, I can't seem to find the true owner of that short and bold statement. While men may claim ownership of the world, there is no doubt that women are the ones who make it run smoothly.

In an article, that was dedicated to mothers, by the late, great Pulitzer Prize-winning film critic, Roger Ebert, he shared the many ways that women are just plain better than men. When I read his article, I was surprised that he made absolutely no references or comparisons to women in movies, just his own raw and real observations, about how women rock, and make the world a much better place.

Below is a quick summary of Roger's key points for his piece. They're full of generalizations, but his hypotheses are still intuitively true:

o Women tend to exhibit more kindness, empathy, and generosity compared to men, making them well-suited for leadership positions.
o Violent crimes and crimes in general are far less likely to involve women.
o Women are (statistically) safer drivers.

o In a single-parent household, a child is more likely to have better outcomes if the parent is a woman.

"Because we do not often think of ourselves as animals, it is rather wonderful that women retain one function from their evolutionary past. They have breasts and use them to feed infants. Think about that. In terms of body weight, they tend to have larger breasts than most mammals, although breast size has no particular relationship to feeding ability. One obvious reason for larger breasts, therefore, is to send a signal to prospective mates that they are promising candidates for motherhood. You may not realize this when you see a crowd of half-loaded guys in a lap-dance joint, but in some primeval sense they're looking for mothers - perhaps their own."

o A woman is more willing to marry an ugly man, than a man is to marry an ugly woman. The woman is looking for reliability, responsibility, and security from a man. Men tend to look for a woman with nice boobs.

o In business, women are not as quick as men to grow enraged at the idea of raising the hourly wage. For most men, the minimum wage is important largely because of its impact on profits. Women consider minimum wage for its effect on helping wage-earners support their families.

o Men's sports can be brutish. For example, athletes suffering brain damage in the process of winning a "big game" like the Superbowl, is a price (mainly male) team owners are only too willing to pay.

o Men and religion. This topic could be a book unto itself. It would seem that the God of all humans can be approached only through men. Judaism, Christianity, and Islam were founded by patriarchal desert tribes, and male supremacy was reflected in their theology. In many fundamentalist sects, wives are taught to be subservient to their husbands and "to obey." Catholics, Muslims, and traditional Jews restrict their priesthoods to men.

o Women value common welfare above singular success and are more open to cooperation than competition. Women have evolved to focus more on prudent long-term survival, and less on immediate gains.

"When women give birth and spend months suckling an infant, they understand better that we all depend on each other. They're programmed to nurture the defenseless, plan for the future, and value others for their qualities, rather than for their externals."

All I can say is, *'Roger that,'* Roger!

After a particularly difficult week of frustrating interactions with both of my ex-husbands, I asked a wise old bird (aka my mother) why men are so damned useless? With a straight face, she answered, *"Oh dear, it's a new era we live in. Environmentalism is all the rage."*

With a puzzled look on my face, but still somehow expecting great wisdom from a woman who has been on this earth for a long, long while, I asked her to clarify. She went on to tell me that many people these days are very conscientious of the amount of waste they contribute to the overflowing landfills, and *"Wouldn't the world be a better place if we all just used less?"* Sitting on that for a moment, I was relieved to notice the almost empty bottle of red wine on the coffee table, and also that my mom was distracted - immersed in her favourite (albeit useless) show, *The Bachelor*. So rather than diagnose my mom with certain dementia, and cruelly commit her to a long-term care facility, mid-season, I gave her thoughtless response some actual thought.

Maybe men really are "conservationists." They certainly advocate for the protection and preservation of their familiar and comfortable environment (also known as their "comfort zone") - by resisting change and shifting much of life's heavy lifting onto us. And maybe their uselessness is actually just a clever ploy to keep us women in their lives, on our toes, and helping them to feel safe and secure.

The best bit of gossip at any girls-only dinner table revolves around slagging our hubbies, boyfriends, bosses, and all of our other useless male acquaintances. Our bitching about men can go on for hours, and it's become an acceptable form of entertainment. Honestly, what would we have to talk about (and complain about) if our men were self-sufficient, and they weren't calling us or texting every ten minutes, asking *"When will you be home?"* or *"Jimmy Jr. needs you - he doesn't like me as well as Mommy,"*etc., etc. And although we cry and complain about our men, *"till the cows come home,"* it's obvious that their uselessness gives us great purpose.

Because life imitates art, we can sometimes feel like a character in our own dramatic movie. But whether we're losing ourselves in a good film, spending quality time with other women, or just taking a moment to catch our breath and step back, we all need a temporary escape to appreciate the useless men we let into our lives.